PLANTS FOR
PROBLEM
PLACES

PLANTS FOR PROBLEM PLACES

GRAHAM RICE

TIMBER PRESS
Portland, Oregon

Line illustrations by David Henderson

Paperback edition published in 1995 by
Timber Press, Inc.
The Haseltine Building
133 S.W. Second Avenue, Suite 450
Portland, Oregon 97204, U.S.A.

Printed in Hong Kong

Library of Congress Cataloging-in-Publication Data

Rice, Graham.
    Plants for problem places/Graham Rice.
        p.   cm.
    Bibliography: p.
    Includes index.
    ISBN 0-88192-314-1 (paperback)
    1. Gardening. 2. Plants, Ornamental. I. Title.
SB453.R52   1988   87-27465
635.9—dc 19   CIP

CONTENTS

ACKNOWLEDGEMENTS

First, I'd like to thank Sue for putting up with me while I was writing this book and for reading and commenting on the manuscript. Thanks again to my Mum, for her invaluable comments on my occasionally eccentric grammar and other stylistic quirks, and to John Plummer of Piano Pie Productions for his medal-winning Plants for Problem Places garden at the Chelsea Flower Show.

Most of the photographs are my own but I must also thank Bressingham Gardens for permission to reproduce pictures of two of their introductions, Phil Lusby for one and *Practical Gardening* magazine for a further four pictures. The excellent line drawings are by David Henderson.

I must also thank Jo, Melanie, Ann and everyone at Christopher Helm (including the man himself) with whom it's a pleasure to work.

Finally, thank you to the long suffering Mike Wyatt, editor of *Practical Gardening*, for the title of the book.

INTRODUCTION

We all have problems. It's an illusion to think that somewhere there's a person with a problem free life. And the dream of one day being rid of all our troubles will not lead, eventually, to perfect happiness but to the constant, niggling dissatisfaction with life which threatens our peace of mind. The trick is to acknowledge that our lives will never be perfect and then to get on with the fun.

And there's no such thing as the problem free garden any more than there's a problem free life. Every garden has its difficulties, and if we think that with just one change or the introduction of just one new technique it can be made perfect, then we will be constantly striving for the unattainable. Rather, we must realise that, for example, we will never be able to grow swathes of rhododendrons if we garden on limestone. We must just enjoy all the wonderful plants that will give us pleasure in our particular situation.

So, this is a book about realism, about looking at the inevitable problems that face every gardener, thinking constructively on how to alleviate them and then, having reduced their impact, choosing plants to give us lasting enjoyment.

I've picked out 13 factors which gardeners see as problems and first of all described their characteristics. In one or two cases this has meant saying that there really is not a problem. Gardeners with wet soil may not be able to grow choice alpines without a huge amount of work but at least they can grow the wonders of ligularias and bog primulas. The second part of each chapter suggests how the problem can be alleviated to enable as wide a range of plants to be grown as possible and, finally, there are the plants themselves.

In most chapters I have divided the section on plants into five parts — trees; hedges; shrubs and climbers; perennials, and annuals. In each part I've described a selection of the plants that will thrive in the given situation and have followed with a short list of others worth considering. I've tried to ensure that there's as little duplication as possible so that if a plant is described in one chapter it will rarely turn up in another. This may mean that some good plants are not described under the heading where you may expect to find them if they are especially useful in more than one situation.

At the end of each description there is a little code such as z5 or z8. American readers will recognise this as a reference to the zones by which plants are coded according to their hardiness — the lower the number the tougher they are. This system is useful for British readers, too, and maps explaining it will be found on pp. 175–7.

Obviously, my experience does not extend to gardening on all the soils and in all the situations covered in this book so I have sometimes referred to the wisdom of others with different experience. Some of their books are mentioned in the bibliography.

Finally, can I say that no problem is so bad that it must defeat us totally. Even the most impossible conditions can be improved to the extent that we can grow many attractive plants. It may be that we won't be able to grow our especial favourites in the spots that suit them least. Although we must strive for the perfect, we must be satisfied with what is possible.

1

NEW GARDENS

THE PROBLEM

Looking out of the kitchen window on a new plot can be very daunting, especially for the less than expert gardener. It may look like a fresh canvas just awaiting the brush but there are hidden problems. Quite how many depends on circumstances but one or maybe all of the following difficulties may occur.

If the house is a new one there's no telling how conscientious the builders have been during its construction. What is certain is that their equipment will have run back and forth over the soil compacting it severely and often destroying the natural drainage.

Another problem with new developments is what exactly the builders have hidden away under the covering of soil. Sometimes they have acted responsibly and removed all their debris. But when you start to dig you may well find that a surprising variety of rubbish turns up. Bricks and rubble are common but I've also heard of pipes, long lengths of wire and chain link fence, huge lumps of concrete, old boots and jackets, even the foreman's teapot. It's a sad fact that it pays to investigate fairly thoroughly before starting to work on the garden, for it's very dispiriting to lay a lawn and then when you come to dig the borders find that there's an old concrete post buried in the border and under the lawn as well, so that you have to dig up your new grass to remove it.

The soil that covers the rubbish is often less than perfect as the layers get moved during construction and the rough subsoil may end up on the surface. This soil may be of low fertility and may also contain large numbers of weed seeds which have been in the soil for many years just waiting to leap up and smother everything you plant.

A completely different problem is that, regardless of the soil, a new garden looks very bare and many plants take some time to achieve sufficient bulk to make an impression on the scene. Without trees, substantial shrubs and hedges a garden presents but a bleak prospect so there's a lot of work to do, and maybe some time to wait, before your horticultural dreams will come true.

Then there's the finance. Most people when they move into a new house have spent most of their funds and what little is left goes on decorating it to their taste and on small improvements. This leaves very little for the garden and so economical methods have to be employed to ensure that beds and borders can be planted quickly.

Gardening often has to be economical in terms of time too, when work on a new house (or working overtime to pay for it) has to be given priority. So plants chosen in the early years have to be able to look after themselves.

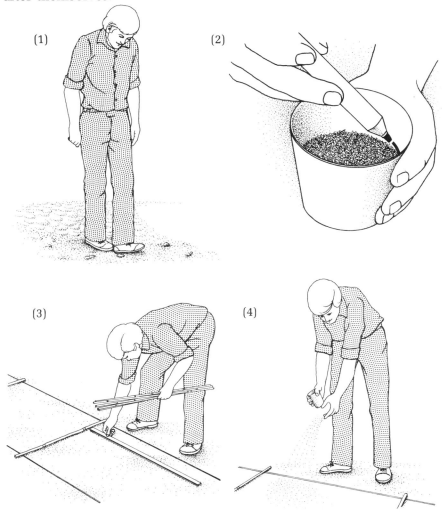

Sowing lawn seed. *Fork and tread the area well (1), fill a measure with the correct amount of seed for a square yard and make a mark (2), mark out the area into square yards (3), sprinkle a measure of seed on each area (4).*

ALLEVIATING THE PROBLEM

There are two ways of coping with builders' debris in your soil — dig it out or leave it where it is. Of course, going back a stage, the clever gardener takes a spade when looking at a new house and digs a few exploratory holes in the garden to find out what's there. Although your findings may prove useful when it comes to negotiating on the price, it's unlikely that you'll persuade the builder to dig it up again and provide you with good topsoil instead.

Digging it all out is no fun. However if there's not too much it's probably the best way to cope. Attack a small area first, improve the soil — or add good topsoil to it if you need to, and then plant it up at once so you can see you've achieved something. Then when that's done move on to the next area.

Only decide to leave all, or most of it, where it is if it doesn't come too near the surface. If there's 9in (23cm) of reasonable soil present that's enough to make a lawn, and it might pay to let the presence of dumped hardcore or old bricks influence, at least to a limited extent, the exact area of a patio or drive.

Raised beds can be useful if the amount of hardcore and the like is too much to contemplate moving it — as it is on a few occasions. They can provide a sufficient depth of soil to grow almost any plants you like although you will need some good soil to make the basis of the mix that goes in the raised area.

Some things must be removed. Patches of soil where oil or other noxious liquids have been spilled should be dug out and the soil taken to the dump or otherwise disposed of; don't be tempted to spread it around the garden and dig it in. Wire mesh is best removed because if it's spread over a wide area it will be constantly infuriating.

Summing up, the best advice is this:

1. Check the garden before you buy the house.
2. Try and site sheds, greenhouses, patios, drives and sandpits on the worst areas.
3. Dig out and discard any soil soaked with noxious liquids.
4. Remove as much of the debris as possible, especially wire, from areas which are to be beds and borders.
5. Ensure that at least 9in (23cm) of soil remains over areas to be grassed.
6. Build raised beds if the problem in some areas is insoluble.

Compaction is also a problem which can demand a lot of work to cure effectively. Many of the answers will be found in Chapter 12 on waterlogged soils, as waterlogging is the chief feature of such conditions. If the problem is not too severe single digging will loosen the top 9in (23cm) of soil and a rotary cultivator can be a great help on lighter soils (but beware of the debris!). More substantial compaction may demand double digging.

Low fertility can be greatly improved by the addition of large quantities of organic matter. Constant attention to weed control may be necessary too — unfortunately this doesn't always fit in with the need to spend relatively little time on the garden. So just take on a little at a time.

The problem of the garden looking bare for some years can be solved by choosing vigorous and fast growing plants which will speedily fill the space, and in particular shrubs which quickly make a good size.

The garden can be planted economically by choosing plants which can be split soon after planting, can be easily increased from cuttings or can be raised from seed in substantial quantities.

SOLVING THE PROBLEM WITH PLANTS

Trees

Laburnum The laburnum is chosen for new gardens for its tolerance of a wide variety of disagreeable conditions. It makes a small tree festooned in late spring or early summer in hanging clusters of yellow pea flowers. This is a tree that seeds itself about generously but this facility is of no comfort to the gardener as when the seedlings first flower they will be seen to be very poor indeed.

There is another problem, though one which may have been overexaggerated, and that is that the seeds are poisonous; it's therefore frequently suggested that it not be planted where there are children. Although children are obviously not in the habit of scraping up handfuls of seeds from the soil and swallowing them, this danger must be considered if there are going to be children around.

However, there is a solution and it happens to be a pleasant one. *Laburnum* × *watereri* 'Vossii' is one of the best varieties for flowers, producing them in generous quantities and in long strings and this variety has the extra bonus of producing very few seeds. So you will not be bothered by seedlings popping up and the difficulty of resisting the temptation to keep them, and children will be safe, too. There is also a lovely weeping variety sometimes seen which is equally unlikely to produce seed, *L.* × *watereri* 'Alford's Weeping'. z6

Lime (Tilia) That the lime is often used as a street tree where it suffers from far worse damage to the soil than ever occurs in a garden shows that it can cope with adverse conditions. In the wild it occurs mainly on limestone but seems a little less fussy in gardens.

A substantial tree making an elegant, broadly spreading crown with sweetly scented flowers in summer. This is not a tree for small gardens

4

but one which will grace a larger plot on inhospitable soil as long as its planting site is well prepared.

The small-leaved lime, *Tilia cordata*, is eventually a large tree with an attractive habit and sweetly scented summer flowers. There is a good narrow headed variety, 'Green Spire'. The broad leaved lime, *T. platyphyllos*, is more vigorous and eventually a little larger. This too has a more upright version, 'Rubra', which is also distinguished by its red twigs.

These limes, although establishing well in relatively inhospitable conditions, do make large trees and it may be necessary to contemplate their removal after 15 years, during which time the fertility of the soil will, I hope, have been improved; then something more choice and lastingly manageable can be planted. z4

Also try. . . Betula pendula, Sorbus aria, Robinia pseudacacia

Hedges

Privet (Ligustrum) Much planted and much despised, it has to be said that the privet does make a good hedge if looked after and, although it has its faults, it will quickly make a good barrier in difficult situations. *Ligustrum ovalifolium* and its golden variety 'Aureum' are the ones usually planted. The problems with privet are a tendency to bareness at the base if the young plants are not cut back hard on planting and again fairly hard later in the year. There's also the hungry root system to cope with and they need clipping regularly. But they're about the cheapest form of hedging and I once heard of someone who planted two privet hedges as windbreaks and then removed them after a few years when other plants had grown up. z5

Leyland's cypress (× Cupressocyparis leylandii) This is included here by way of a warning. The Leyland's cypress is a hybrid tree which was first planted in 1892 and as far as I know the original trees are still growing. Those which are at present the tallest are growing in south west England and were not planted until 1916 but are, even so, over 100ft (31m) high. In summer this tree can grow 4in (10cm) in a week; so when considering planting it as a hedge the fact that it's so extraordinarily vigorous must be considered. It's all very well saying that it reaches the required size quickly, so it does, but it doesn't stop there. So beware, a hedge of Leyland's cypress is more likely to create problems than solve them. z6

Also try. . . Lupinus arboreus, Sambucus varieties, Symphoricarpus × chenaultii

Shrubs

Clematis montana This most beautiful and most accommodating of climbers is a vigorous plant for a north, west or east wall or fence where it can be given plenty of space — which it will soon occupy. In spring it will then give a delightful display of four-petalled pink flowers. Like forsythia, this is a plant which is despised for being often planted and easy to grow but this is very unfair. The best varieties to look for are 'Elisabeth' in a very soft pink and 'Rubens' in a darker pink with purplish buds. z5

Hypericum The big yellow flowers which are a feature of most hypericums are especially fine on two varieties *Hypericum* 'Hidcote' (z7) and *H. calycinum* (z6), plants very different in their manner of growth. 'Hidcote' is a shrub reaching about 5ft (1.5m) with dark foliage and big brilliant yellow flowers all summer. This is a tough and reliable shrub for most soils. *H. calycinum*, the rose of Sharon, is a creeping ground cover plant reaching only about 12–15in (30–38cm) high for sun or shade, wet or dry conditions with even bigger flowers making a stunning summer sight when grown in large patches. But its season is not long and for the rest of the year it's sadly unremarkable.

Lavatera olbia A short-lived plant but one which grows very quickly, soon making a substantial plant. This is one of the indispensable new garden plants for not only does it make a large plant in double quick time but it's cheap to buy and when you have it you can raise plenty more from cuttings. It's upright in growth and its greyish foliage sets off big pink hollyhock-like flowers. A well-drained soil in a sunny spot suits it best. To prolong the life of the plant it pays to cut the shoots back by half in autumn to prevent wind damage and then prune hard in spring. z8

Leycesteria formosa A demure plant but one which puts up happily with poor unimproved soil to make a modest display. This is a small shrub, upright in growth with stout branches which carry pendulous heads of white flowers in summer. These are set amongst purplish green bracts and are followed by dark fruits which are eaten by birds and so distributed about the garden. z7

Tree lupin (Lupinus arboreus) Now here's an underrated plant if ever there was one. Wild in California and naturalised in Britain this is another short-lived shrub for better-drained soils. Again it has a number of qualities particularly in demand in new gardens. It grows quickly, it makes a very showy shrub, it's cheap to buy or it can easily be raised from seed.

The tree lupin rapidly grows into a rounded bush of pretty fingered foliage with, in the best varieties, long spikes of bright yellow flowers.

Some of the seed raised mixtures are rather poor with watery purples and dirty whites — it's the pure, bright yellow which is the most exciting. z7

Mock orange (Philadelphus) For scent in late spring there's little to beat the white purity of philadelphus. It's generally an upright growing shrub which can vary in size from 2–6ft (0.6–1.8m) and in late spring the white flowers, single or double, appear. 'Manteau d'Hermine' is a dwarf one with dense, twiggy growth and double, strongly scented flowers, while 'Belle Etiole' is larger and a little more lax with single flowers blushed with pink at the centre. 'Virginal' is the showiest of all, a large shrub with big pure white flowers and strong scent.

The larger types in particular are strong growers and all will tolerate less than ideal conditions. z4

Stag's horn sumach (Rhus typhina) Some people like this for the curious antler-like effect of the winter shoots but I grow it for its autumn colour. And there's only one variety for this purpose, *Rhus typhina* 'Laciniata'.

It usually makes a broad shrub with only a few branches which are rather downy. The leaves are long and finely cut and in the autumn are brilliantly coloured in red, orange and yellow — quite magnificent. Although perfectly accommodating, the stag's horn sumach does have a tendency to sucker badly, especially if the roots are damaged by the hoe, so beware when removing weeds from under and around it. Once the suckers start it's difficult to stop them. This is a good ground covering shrub while young for, although it produces few branches, the foliage cover is dense. z3

Flowering currant (Ribes sanguineum) With forsythia, one of the most popular of spring-flowering shrubs. The pendulous strings of pink or red flowers appear just as the foliage is shooting on substantial shrubs which survive well in most conditions. Unfortunately, the flowers smell rather unpleasant, as if a cat has forgotten its training in the area.

'Pulborough Scarlet' is the best variety and is sometimes planted alternately with *Forsythia* 'Lynwood' on fences. It's quick growing and although tending to upward sweeping branches makes a big shrub quickly and can also be easily increased by hardwood cuttings. z5

Rubus 'Benenden' Few gardeners think of growing a cane fruit for its flowers but, in effect, that's what I'm recommending. This is a relative of the blackberry and raspberry, though without the spines, grown for its large, single, white flowers which are scented and line the tall arching shoots in spring. A vigorous shrub which fills out quickly and tolerates a wide range of adverse conditions, including neglect. z6

Weigela One of the first plants I put in my present garden was a 'Bristol Ruby' which soon grew so big that I had to move it. The problem with it and most of the other varieties is that the foliage is dull, a rough green, so that after the deep red flowers in spring there's little to look forward to until the following year. Apart from 'Bristol Ruby', varieties to look out for are 'Eva Rathke' which is slower in growth and has crimson flowers and 'Abel Carriere' which is paler.

Rather different is *Weigela florida* 'Variegata', a fine shrub with white edges to the leaves which in spring provides just the right background to the pink flowers. When the flowers are over the variegation is attractive for the rest of the summer. z5

Also try. . . Amelanchier lamarkii, Buddlia davidii varieties, Cornus alba, Cotoneaster, Olearia haastii

Perennials

Achillea ptarmica Some gardeners think of this as an invasive weed but in relatively unimproved soils its habits will be modified somewhat and anyway, in a new garden, what's wrong with a plant that spreads quickly to fill a good space? It reaches about 2ft (60cm) and in the best varieties its upright stems are topped with heads of densely double white flowers. 'The Pearl' is the most often seen and can be raised from seed and then divided almost every year once planted. 'Perry's White' is whiter and a little taller. z3

Bugle (Ajuga) Indispensable carpeters for sun or shade with spikes of blue, or rarely pink, flowers in spring. Varieties come with a range of foliage shades from bronze to white variegated but the naming of some of the dark ones is a little confused. 'Atropurpurea' has darker than beetroot foliage and blue flowers; 'Burgundy Glow' has pink marks, a creamy edge and pale blue flowers; 'Multicolor' has dark bronze foliage irregularly splashed with pink and cream; the less vigorous 'Variegata' has almost white edges to its greyish green leaves and is a little more shy to flower.

They all spread well as long as the soil is not too dry and pieces can be detached regularly and replanted to expand the size of the group rapidly. All the varieties are attractive so order all those I've mentioned and any more you come across. z4

Delphinium Stately plants for the back of the border in sun or a little shade and most soils. It's now possible to raise a variety of types from seed economically and these range from the relatively dwarf 'Blue Fountains' at about 3ft (90cm) in various blues, purples, lilacs and white to the 'Pacific Giants' reaching twice the height with flowers in the same range. The rather newer 'Dreaming Spires' sometimes has pinkish and greenish shades amongst its colours.

If treated as half-hardy annuals almost all varieties will produce at least one flower spike in the first summer and then a very generous crop in the second year. z3

Leopard's bane (Doronicum) Another good perennial to raise from seed and another that cheerfully produces its big bright yellow daisies on 18in (45cm) stems, in a variety of unreasonable conditions. This is one of the first of the more flamboyant perennials to flower in the spring, its leaves are a fresh and cheerful green and as long as it gets a little sun it seems happy in most soils.

Doronicum cordatum 'Magnificum' (z3) can be raised from seed easily and will divide after a year or two as well. There's also 'Miss Mason' (z4) and the double-flowered 'Spring Beauty' (z4) varieties which are increased only by division.

Cranesbill (Geranium) Certain of these amenable perennials are ideal new garden plants being tough and fairly vigorous and some are also good weed suppressors. Geranium pratense (z5) is one of the tallest and most vigorous reaching 3ft (90cm) and spreading well. The leaves are deeply divided and very attractive, the open flowers are light blue. This plant has a tendency to self-sow rather aggressively so the double varieties, such as the pale blue 'Caeruleum Plenum', may be better choices if you don't want the whole border choked in a few years. The individual plants spread well making a dense cover.

'Claridge Druce' (z6) is also vigorous though maybe a little shorter and rapidly colonises large areas with its slightly greyish foliage and magenta flowers all summer. 'Wargrave Pink' (z3) is altogether less strident both in colour and habits.

Lupins (Lupinus) Almost all lupins are now raised from seed and this is a cheap and quick way of raising these wonderful plants. If treated as half-hardy annuals they will flower in their first summer and then again far more impressively the following year. They can also be sown outside in early summer and moved into their final homes in the autumn. It's not easy to divide them but as seed is widely available it doesn't really matter.

The best of the taller types reaching about 4ft (1.2m) is 'Band of Nobles', an improved selection of the old Russell lupins that are still so well remembered. On a smaller scale 'Lulu' at about 2ft (60cm) is excellent and both come in a good range of colours. These are essential early summer plants and should be grown in large quantities so that plenty are available for cutting. z4

Polygonum bistorta This is such a good coloniser for any soils that are not too dry that new gardeners will, I hope, forgive its lack of punch. Indeed it should help foster an appreciation of the subtle and sublime so essential to the enjoyment of plants.

Weigela 'Bristol Ruby' is a tough and reliable plant for new gardens, flowering when young and tolerating poor conditions.

Large numbers of Lilium regale can be raised from seed easily and Salvia superba can be increased quickly from cuttings.

Spreading well, too well in the relatively small border where I have it, it produces a dense cover of broad leaves from which rise tall wiry stems topped with cylindrical heads of pink flowers. Cut off the heads as they fade for more flowers later. New plants can appear up to 2ft (60cm) from the parent plant as the roots creep stealthily underground and then surprise you. z3

Salvia superba More correctly known as S. *nemerosa* 'Superba', this is one of the best and longest flowering of border perennials partly because the purple bracts amongst the flowers are still colourful for a long time after the flowers have actually dropped. It reaches about 3ft (90cm), is easily increased from early cuttings and harmonises well with many other plants. The variety 'Lubecca' at half the height is much more compact if you prefer it. z5

Tansy (Tanacetum vulgare) The ordinary form is not worth any space as an ornamental plant but there's a variety with finely divided ferny foliage called 'Crispum' which is much more appealing. It makes stiff, upright stems about 3ft (90cm) high with the darkest green dissected foliage and this is topped in summer with small yellow button flowers. The problem is that although it's happy in any soil and any site, wherever you plant it, it spreads — in three years mine spread from one plant of three shoots to a clump 4ft (1.2m) across. This is ideal if you want to fill the space, but not otherwise. z3

Also try... Lamium maculatum, Pulmonaria officinalis, Vinca species

Annuals and Bedding Plants

Marguerite (Chrysanthemum) The shrubby chrysanthemums are frost-tender bedding plants which in most areas are kept in a frost-free greenhouse in winter and planted out for the summer. The have double or single daisy flowers in a range of colours on large rounded bushes. My favourite is the Paris daisy, *Chrysanthemum foeniculaceum*, with finely cut grey foliage and single white daisies. The rather more coarse *C. frutescens* comes in a single white but there is also a version with a large pink centre, 'Mary Wooton', but it's the vigorous and long-flowering single yellow, 'Jamaica Primrose', which really takes the prize. A wonderful plant covered in flower all summer and spreading well. All are best in the sun.

They are easily raised from cuttings and if just one plant is kept frost-free over the winter you will soon build up a substantial stock during the spring.

Shrubby chrysanthemums like the yellow 'Jamaica Primrose' and this 'Vancouver' make broad spreading bushes very quickly.

Geranium (Pelargonium) The bedding geranium is one of the best summer plants for sunny spots whatever the soil. As long as it gets a good start it will flower all summer. It has to be said that some of the new seed-raised hybrids are less good at tolerating poor conditions than their cuttings-raised progenitors but amongst the seed-raised ones go for 'Red Elite', a good scarlet, 'Picasso', an unusual magenta, and for good ground cover try 'Breakaway Red' and 'Breakaway Salmon'.

Marigold (Tagetes) More toughies for sunny spots, the African and French types are both good. Although the modern hybrids are excellent they are expensive compared with older types which provide a brilliant display at a very reasonable price. Varieties like the African 'Crackerjack Mixed' in a variety of orange and yellow shades and the French 'Naughty Marietta', a single yellow with a red blotch, will give sheets of colour from just one packet of seed as long as they are given sunshine and a reasonable start.

Also try. . . Chrysanthemum carinatum, Eschscholtzia californica, Iberis umbellata

2

WINDY GARDENS

THE PROBLEM

Gardeners sometimes feel faced with an impossible choice between living in a sheltered frost pocket or on a windy hill. But even if you choose the hollow, wind can still plague you. Not wind on the grand scale but wind funnelled by buildings and hedges to create a local blast which can be just as damaging.

So there is wind on a grand scale and wind on a local scale. Wind on a grand scale can be exceptionally destructive — it can demolish a stone wall with one blast, so tall plants won't have much of a chance and you can often see the effect on wild trees which are wind pruned, that is, the buds on the windward side are seared off so that the tree grows at an angle away from the blast.

Greenhouses can be severely damaged especially if the ventilators or doors are left open as this gives the wind something to tug at. Cloches are very susceptible, I remember looking out of an upstairs window one morning to see the new cloches I had on trial from a manufacturer bouncing across a sugar beet field — closely followed by my washing. Large trees can be uprooted or branches broken off causing damage to the house and garden and, of course, smaller plants can be broken.

But damage can also be caused in ways less immediately obvious. When a dry wind passes over the surface of a leaf it picks up the water vapour that the leaf is naturally giving off. The drier the wind and the faster it travels the more moisture it picks up. Young foliage can lose water at such a rate that it quickly dries and shrivels. In extreme conditions older foliage and the foliage of especially susceptible plants can suffer in the same way. If the soil is very dry or frozen, in a protracted windy period the situation could be even more serious. Plants cannot take up water from frozen or very dry soil, so the moisture lost through the leaves cannot be replenished. Water is drawn from other parts of the plant and eventually the plant, or parts of the plant, dies of drought.

Another less apparent result of windy conditions is that it prevents pollinating insects from working. Unpollinated fruit trees crop unexpectedly badly under what would otherwise be ideal conditions; it can be a problem with a few vegetables too, seed is not set on flowers; and there may be a reduced display on shrubs grown for their ornamental fruits. And, of course, you can't spray against pests in windy conditions.

More obviously, trees can be affected by wind rock so that their roots never get a hold. Shrubs can be rocked at the root too. Tall herbaceous plants can be easily broken, the flower heads of bulbs snapped off, fruit can be blown off trees, mulches can be blown away entirely. Trees with delicate blossom, like flowering cherries, and many poppies can have their petals blown away almost before the flowers open. Fences as well as walls can be blown over and this is especially common where the posts are inadequate for the size and type of fence. Climbers may be unceremoniously dumped in the border.

ALLEVIATING THE PROBLEM

If you're a keen gardener probably the first advice to remember is to try and buy a house and garden in a sheltered spot. But having said that, the garden at Inverewe on the west coast of Scotland, which is on an exceptionally windy site, should be an inspiration.

Shelter must be the first priority. And ideally this needs to be in the form of trees and shrubs rather than walls. A wall creates a great deal of turbulence on its leeward side which can itself be damaging but a belt of trees and shrubs filters and softens the wind creating little or no turbulence. The science of farm shelterbelts was once highly

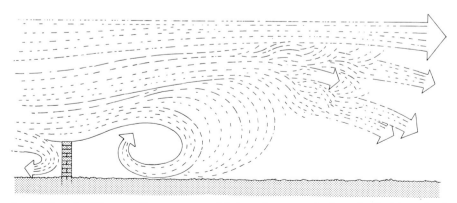

A solid barrier like a wall can cause eddying of strong winds on both sides which may damage plants.

developed but some of its principles can also be applied to protecting gardens. The protection given by a line of trees is directly proportional to the height of the trees and is summarised in the following table.

Distance from shelterbelt	Approximate percentage reduction in wind speed
2 × height of shelterbelt	75
5	66
10	50
15	20
20	15
30	10

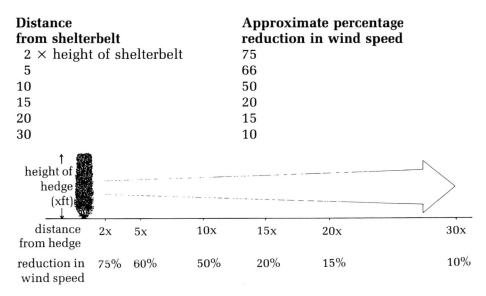

distance from hedge	2x	5x	10x	15x	20x	30x
reduction in wind speed	75%	60%	50%	20%	15%	10%

Wind speed is reduced immediately behind a hedge but then increases.

This applies as much to garden hedges as to larger shelterbelts.

Planting a shelterbelt is not just a matter of putting in a row of trees. To give the very best protection, and probably improve on the approximate figures given in the table, a shelterbelt needs to be planned carefully. The first thing to remember is that when trees are planted fairly closely together as they are in a shelterbelt they tend to become bare of lower branches. So, ideally, a row of shorter trees or large shrubs should also be planted. In fact the ideal arrangement is for a row of large, dense bushy shrubs on the windward side, then the main protective planting of trees and then a gradually diminishing range of smaller trees and large shrubs. This will reduce turbulence and give the maximum filtration.

On a garden scale this must be greatly modified for there just isn't the space to plant so thoroughly. A single row of large evergreen shrubs or small trees is usually sufficient and this can be supplemented by internal hedges to beef up the decline in protection shown in the table.

The other thing to remember is that when wind meets a barrier, as well as attempting to filter through, it will try and sweep round the edge, so that if at all possible a shelterbelt should extend beyond the area to be protected.

When the trees or shrubs are first planted they, too, will need help in the early stages when they will be subjected to the intensity of the blast from which they will eventually be sheltering other plants. Adequate staking is vital and research has shown that short stakes are actually more beneficial to the tree than traditional long stakes. Evergreens will also need protection from the wind until they become established and a barrier of plastic mesh windbreak material which, like trees and shrubs, filters the wind will make a substantial difference to the rate of establishment of the plants.

In more local situations, in the garden itself and in urban or village areas where the consideration of shelterbelts is impossible, planting can also help. If you already have a wall then you will know all about the turbulence that I've already mentioned. If you can arrange to plant a hedge immediately outside the wall, depending on who actually owns the land, this can help. It sounds mad, planting a hedge alongside a wall, but it will so reduce the impact of the wind on the wall that turbulence will be dramatically reduced. Of course, wall shrubs would do just as well but they have to be tough and bushy. It will also reduce the wind speed on the windward side of the wall which may help to persuade the owner.

This beneficial effect works on the windward side as well as the leeward side, especially of hedges. The reduction is not dramatic but at a distance from the hedge of twice its height there can be a reduction of 25 per cent.

So, if you have a wall, plant a hedge or wall shrubs on the windward side as this will reduce the turbulence and wind speed on both sides of the wall. If the wind whistles round the corner of the house — and it usually speeds up in such a situation — a judiciously planted conifer or two, or other evergreen shrubs, can make all the difference.

Once you start to think about the garden itself there's still a lot that can be done to lessen the destructive influence of strong wind. Hedges within the garden are an obvious solution, of course, but then there is always the competition from their roots for water and plant nutrients plus what may be unwanted shade. So it's often a better idea to plant either groups of substantial but ornamental shrubs or to plant cordon fruit trees as windbreaks. It's true that cordon fruit will not have the effect of a hedge but you may be able to plant more than one row and, after all, they are productive.

Then, of course, you can always support the plants. Dahlias, delphiniums, cimicifugas — there are many plants which according to the degree of protection you can give them may or may not need support. The secret is to secure them unobtrusively so that the supports do not detract from the effect and also to do it in good time. However, staking too early can also be unsatisfactory as the display is made up of sticks for as long as it's made up of flowers! But it must not be left until the plants flop for a resurrected plant is rarely an attractive one.

Opinions differ as to the best methods of staking and to some extent the method you use depends on the materials available. Brushwood, and especially hazel, is the best. Hazel is ideally suited to supporting plants for it grows in such conveniently flat, fan-like sprays. Set around a group you need very few pieces to do a good job and if string is run around and across as well you will have a very efficient support. The tops of the twigs can also be snapped over above the growing shoots as an extra. Birch twigs are sometimes available but they are much less satisfactory.

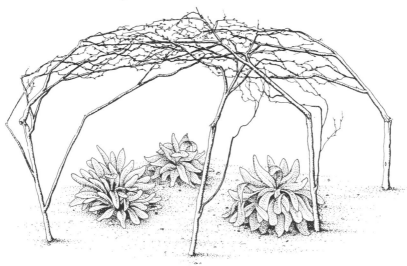

Border plants can be supported by hazel brushwood placed around plants well in advance. Break the tops over to provide extra stability.

Foliage will eventually grow through the twigs and be supported efficiently while hiding the supports.

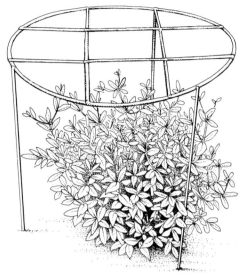

Wire rings also make useful and sturdy supports which last for many years.

When the foliage grows through wire supports it hides the wire well and is supported steadily.

For many of us hazel twigs are difficult to find and we have to resort to canes and string. Four or five bamboo canes are set at the corners of a group and string run around them and between them. It's simple but sometimes rather stiff and often shows all summer. Plastic or metal mesh supports are useful and if these are put in place early in the season the plants grow through the mesh and are very evenly supported. You can make your own by nailing pieces of plastic garden mesh of the right size on to square stakes and knocking the stakes in at the corners of a group.

Plants like delphiniums are best staked by using a single cane to each flower stem, although unless the canes are tall and run right up into the head, the top of the flower spike can snap at the point of the highest tie.

Thoughtful pruning can be constructive, too, and this is especially relevant in relation to vigorous shrubs like roses and buddleias which are usually pruned hard in spring. By leaving all the growth on over the winter there is a lot of top growth for the wind to tear into and branches can be blown off or wind rock can loosen the roots substantially. On roses and other shrubs this sometimes moves the roots to such an extent that a noticeable gap is formed where the stem enters the ground. This can fill with rain or melting snow, which then freezes — doing the plant no good at all.

The answer is to prune in the autumn, but not fully. Cut back the plants by about half so that any die back or frost damage can be dealt with in the spring at the same time as the final, more careful pruning.

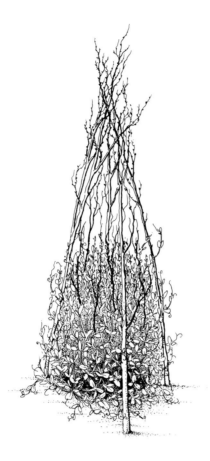

A wigwam of tall brushwood makes an ideal support for annual climbers such as canary creeper and sweet peas.

SOLVING THE PROBLEM WITH PLANTS

If the precautions I've described are taken you will find that so many plants will thrive that I don't have the space to list them. But in some gardens providing really effective shelter is just not possible. So the planting must be very thoughtful.

Plants which grow naturally in woods and humid environments, even if they can thrive in most open borders, are likely to suffer in the wind. Many plants from these situations have never needed to develop tough leaves — ferns are a prime example. Plants with large leaves which are liable to be torn by the wind, like rodgersias, some of the large-leaved hostas, ligularias and the like, are not suitable. Tall plants with top-heavy flower stems like delphiniums are a waste of time unless carefully supported and indeed many tall plants with stems in need of support can break at the ties in spite of being supported.

But there are plants which are ideally suited to windy sites and these are the ones that grow in such situations naturally. Heathers and alpines are the ones that come immediately to mind.

Trees

New Zealand cabbage tree (Cordyline australis) For milder areas only, this palm-like tree forms a tall, stout stem, often with a candelabra-like branching, each branch topped with a dense and striking tuft of long narrow leaves. Flowers do appear and they come in large creamy heads in summer. There's a purple-leaved version, 'Atropurpurea', which is often seen and these trees are a feature of coastal resorts in southern England. They are too tender for other parts of the country. z8

Norway spruce (Picea abies) Now you know what to do with all those old Christmas trees, put them in the windiest spot in the garden. All are suitable, from the dwarf types which are good choices for rock gardens and raised beds to the much more substantial varieties. Apart from the natural species, I would pick out 'Clanbrassiliana' and 'Pyramidalis'.

'Clanbrassiliana' is the one to go on the rock garden, making a broad, flat-topped bush which is very slow growing. The plant at the Hillier Arboretum in Hampshire has still not reached 10ft (3m) across after 40 years. As well as its shape and tiny needles, its brown winter buds are attractive.

'Pyramidalis' is an upright, more compact version of the original forest tree with upward spreading branches and is more suitable where space is limited. z2

Poplar (Populus alba) The Lombardy poplar may be a useful shelter tree but for something a little more ornamental the white poplar, *Populus alba*, is more suitable. The name describes the fluffy white coating on the undersides of the leaves which always makes the tree interesting, especially in windy situations, when the leaves are constantly fluttering. It can make quite a large, broad tree and can sucker, too, so it needs space. There is the additional bonus of yellow autumn colour. The variety 'Richardii' is a lovely tree with bright yellow foliage having the same white wool underneath but it's a great deal less vigorous and may not tolerate the conditions in which its green-leaved relation will revel. There are two more pyramidal versions of the standard white poplar called 'Pyramidalis' and 'Rocket' — the latter is said to be superior but to tell you the truth I haven't compared them. z4

Mountain ash (Sorbus aucuparia) In exposed places this is sometimes the only tree that survives and it is often seen on tops of hills pruned into a strange leaning shape by the wind. In garden situations it is usually spared such treatment but is still a good choice. It's a small tree, suitable for town gardens, with ash-like leaves, clusters of creamy white flowers in spring and the scarlet berries that follow are sometimes on the tree as early as mid summer. There is usually good autumn colour too. 'Asplenifolia' has especially finely cut foliage and good autumn colour, 'Sheerwater Seedling' has berries of a more orangey shade and 'Xanthocarpa' has yellow fruits which the birds tend to leave until last. z3

Also try. . . Acer pseudoplatanus, Alnus glutinosa, Pinus nigra

Shelterbelts

Most of the plants that can be recommended under this heading are so universally tough that they are recommended elsewhere in the book, so here I will do no more than list them. They vary in size and so can be used in the appropriate part of the shelterbelt.

Trees: Norway maple (*Acer platanoides*), p. 136
Sycamore (*Acer pseudoplatanus*), p. 136
Hornbeam (*Carpinus betulus*), p. 153
Beech (*Fagus sylvatica*), p. 139
Mountain pine (*Pinus mugo*)
Austrian pine (*Pinus nigra*)
Corsican pine (*Pinus nigra maritima*), p. 57
Scots pine (*Pinus sylvestris*)
Lombardy poplar (*Populus nigra*), p. 20
Mountain ash (*Sorbus aucuparia*), p. 20
Hawthorn (*Crataegus monogyna*), p. 137

Shrubs: Holly (*Ilex aquifolium*), p. 139
Privet (*Ligustrum ovalifolium*), p. 5
Elder (*Sambucus nigra*), p. 155
Snowberry (*Symphoricarpus*), pp. 24, 80

Hedges

Mountain pine (Pinus mugo) This is an exceptionally tough conifer which grows naturally in some of the coldest mountains in Europe and thrives in most difficult situations. It usually makes a small tree or large shrub with stiff, curved, dark green needles and cones about 2in (5cm) long. There are a number of dwarf types suitable for small hedges, they are excellent wind filterers and also make good hosts to low climbers. If you want a dwarf type go for 'Gnom'. z2

Holm oak (Quercus ilex) The holm or evergreen oak makes a wonderful specimen tree as the avenues at Kew Gardens in London demonstrate and it may seem unreasonable to clip it into a neater shape. But it does make a good sheltering hedge in all but the coldest areas. It can't be kept very small but makes an ideal boundary hedge where wind reduction is crucial. The leaves are glossy on top and covered with greyish down underneath. There are also pale green catkins in late spring and clipping can be done when they're over. z7

Also try. . . Ulex europaeus, Berberis, Ilex

Shrubs

Bamboo (Arundinaria japonica) This is the species most commonly cultivated in the UK and the only one which can be bought easily. It makes very dense thickets of narrow canes more than 10ft (3m) high which often branch sparsely towards the top. Although they are ideal wind depressants they should not be expected to take the full force of the attack, but instead used at strategic points within the garden. Bamboos flower but rarely and, contrary to popular opinion, they do not necessarily die afterwards. This species hardly ever dies. z7

Bladder senna (Colutea arborescens) The yellow pea flowers and the curious, fat, inflated seed pods characterise the bladder senna and they are both attractive and interesting — the pods always cause comment. It's a tall shrub reaching 12ft (3.7m) with divided leaves but not of the most elegant form. It's often rather open in habit so, although it usually puts up with the wind, it tends to filter it through rather than stop it dead. z6

Rose of Sharon (Hypericum calycinum) This is a plant recommended for just about every problem place and is often seen shrivelling rapidly when planted hopefully into dust. This is a shame for it's a beautiful plant if given a chance and near where I live has been used extensively to cover embankments, creating a startling field of yellow in summer. It creeps steadily along making a dense mat of roots but the stems only reach about 15in (38cm) so you have to bend down to look at the delightful flowers in detail — but it's worth it. Give it a good start and it won't look back. z6

Shrubby cinquefoil (Potentilla fruticosa) In Britain this plant grows in shingle in the middle of rivers which gives it a fairly dry and sharply drained surface soil and wet soil down below. But it's the low twiggy nature of the plant which seems to make it a good candidate for resisting wind. Just a few days before writing this, fierce gales swept my garden and apart from removing some panes from the greenhouse also cut off a *Helichrysum siculum* at ground level — the top growth

Even in winter gales tall grasses like this Miscanthus 'Silver Feather' bend attractively without breaking.

Like other varieties, this relatively new pink-flowered Potentilla 'Princess' is a neat and twiggy wind resister.

vanished completely. My potentillas are unscathed.

At one time *Potentilla fruticosa* came only in yellows and oranges, and pretty plants for sun and fairly well-drained soils they are. They flower for most of the summer with five-petalled flowers like flat buttercups which appear almost prolifically in early summer. 'Elizabeth' is a primrose yellow, 'Tangerine' is more or less the colour its name implies while 'Daydawn' is more peachy.

More recently a number of new colours have appeared, including especially the scarlet 'Red Ace' which is less floriferous than the yellow types and needs a little shade to prevent bleaching. There's also 'Princess' in pale pink which often seems to bleach to white in sunny spots. z4

Spanish broom (Spartium junceum) Yet another member of the pea family, this is a plant which actually benefits from the wind. In sheltered gardens it can get rather tall and scraggy but the wind tends to encourage a bushy character and a better show of flowers. An overprotected plant has less going for it as the flowers appear high up where you can't savour their lovely scent. z7

Snowberry (Symphoricarpus orbiculatus) This is a plant which I always seem to be recommending for the least hospitable sites. And this is not because I have a particular penchant for it, far from it. Come to think of it, I don't think I like it much at all! But one shouldn't let one's prejudices get in the way I suppose — although that's the only way to enjoy them! — so here we go with snowberries again. Why not give the variegated version, 'Variegatus', a try? It has purplish fruits which although rather small appear in generous quantities and the variegation consists of an uneven yellow margin to the rather smaller leaf. z2

Gorse (Ulex europaeus) An aggressively spiny shrub familiar in many parts of Britain, especially on poor sandy acid soils. The yellow pea-like flowers are most impressive in spring but as the saying 'kissing's out of season when gorse is out of bloom' implies, there's hardly a month when plants don't have a few flowers. Old plants tend to become very bare at the base but can be cut back hard to encourage fresh growth. Being so fiendishly spiny it pays to choose a site for gorse carefully.

The dwarf *U. minor* flowers mainly in the autumn although the show is still impressive. It needs very dry and poor soil otherwise it grows taller like its inherently larger cousin. z7

Also try. . . Berberis, Ruscus, Sambucus

Perennials

New Zealand burr (Acaena) These wonderful flat carpeters were almost ignored until recently but now they are being more widely grown, for their value is obvious. Almost all creep along the surface of the soil, rooting as they go to a greater or lesser extent. They are grown mainly for their round heads of flower and the burrs that follow.

'Copper Carpet' has greeny copper foliage and slightly reddish flowers and is a reasonably well behaved species, whereas *Acaena pulchella* is very neat and indeed rather slow with pale bronzed leaves. 'Blue Haze' is a lovely bluish-leaved one. I have an all too rampant species which I think is *A. anserinifolia* but all are worth a try and new varieties with improved foliage colour are appearing regularly. They succeed in sun or shade in soils which are not waterlogged. z7

Achillea filipendulina Achilleas do not appear here for the sake of the short alpine types but for the taller border perennials, in particular 'Coronation Gold'. The point is that this is an especially self-supporting plant which will not usually break in strong wind. It will sway and swing but as the flower heads are not bulky, it usually stays intact. This variety grows to about 4ft (1.2m) high with flat heads of yellow flowers over many weeks. z3

Japanese anemone (Anemone × hybrida) I wondered whether this should really find a place here as the wind can sometimes dislodge the petals but this is another swayer rather than a snapper and such a lovely plant that it had to creep in somewhere. My favourite is the pure white 'Honorine Jobert', a classic plant growing to about 4–5ft (1.2–1.5m) with dark green foliage and upright stems which carry the pure flowers; even the buds are attractive. It can be a little invasive and occasionally takes a while to settle down after being divided. There are many others all in white or shades of pink and some which are semi-double and they are all good garden plants which are similarly tolerant of the occasional gale. z5

Miscanthus These very substantial members of the grass family are extremely elegant plants which wave beautifully in the wind even in winter when the stems and foliage have turned a very pale straw shade. They are tall, up to 6ft (1.8m), and are very adaptable but if you want to make sure of the plumy flowers you have to choose the right variety. 'Silver Feather' is the best in a slightly darkish pinkish shade and 'Zebrinus' has unusual cross-leaved yellow variegations and similar flowers. z4

Catmint (Nepeta × faassenii) An excellent association of colours which nature has seen fit to provide in just one plant. Reaching only

Three perennials which survive winds well without staking — Achillea *'Gold Plate'*, Salvia superba *and* Heliopsis.

about 18in (45cm) this catmint has a bushy habit, small grey foliage and lilac flowers in late spring. Of course, it's often spoiled by cats rolling in it overenthusiastically but I'm told you can prevent this by hiding a few spiny rose stems amongst the leaves as this rapidly sends the cats elsewhere. Best in sunny, well-drained sites. z4

Alpine phlox (Phlox subulata) Another creeping carpeter for sunny sites, lying lower on the soil than its familiar relative, *Phlox douglasii*. It makes mossy mats of narrow foliage and in spring the flowers appear — white, pinks and soft blues, even a bright red. Any well-drained site suits these amenable plants and a group of different colours in a great carpet is very appealing, good ground cover and lets the wind just slide over. z3

Stipa gigantea Another tall grass reaching 6ft (1.8m) when in flower in early summer although the foliage only manages about half this height. It looks a little like a huge oat plant although the large flower heads have a very attractive purplish tint at first, later turning to a shining yellow. It thrives in well-drained soil in full sun and waves attractively without snapping. z6

Mullein (Verbascum) Both perennials and biennials fall into this group. They are grown for their broad attractive rosettes of foliage and their spikes of yellow or sometimes white or purple flowers. It's the biennials which have the best rosettes, *Verbascum bombyciferum*

'Silver Lining' in particular is especially white, and although the leaves are large they lay flat so are not usually damaged by gales. The flower heads are tall and covered in white wool with yellow flowers studded all along them. V. *olympicum* is similar although the foliage is a little harder and the flowers a little more golden; it's rather short-lived.

Then there is also V. *phoeniceum*. This is a more reliable perennial and usually comes in a seed-raised mixture of colours including purple, various pinks or white. The rosettes of foliage are dark green rather than silver but still handsome. Separate colours usually need propagating by root cuttings to ensure that they are true to type. Well-drained soil in sun suits them. z6

Also try... Crocosmia species, *Phalaris arundinacea* 'Picta', *Sempervivum* species

Annuals and Bedding Plants

Orache (Atriplex) It's the red-leaved variety, *Atriplex hortensis* 'Rubra', which is the one normally grown and is edible. It's a tall hardy annual, self-sowing prolifically in my garden, with leaves shaped like arrow heads in a bright reddish purple. Although it reaches 5ft (1.5m) in height it waves in the wind very cleverly so rarely gets snapped off.

Quaking grass (Briza) The quaking grass is not only especially attractive in a breeze but also grows contentedly in rather more severe conditions. The heart-shaped heads of papery flowers hang from fine but strong stems and rasp noticeably when ruffled by wind. Quaking grass will seed itself happily in dry sunny places in the garden.

Hawksbeard (Crepis rubra) A delightful upright hardy annual reaching only about 12–18in (30–45cm), the stiff stems are topped in lovely soft pink flowers. If dead-headed regularly it will flower for months from a spring sowing outside and if dead heads are left on towards the end of the summer, self sown seedlings will appear. There's a white version as well.

Violet cress (Ionopsidium acaule) This plant is so small that any gale will blast right over it. Just 2–3in (5–7.5cm) high, it flowers in only a few weeks from sowing. The flowers themselves are violet with a white centre and last for months as the plant slowly gets bigger and floppier — within its own tiny scale. Sunshine and gritty soil suit it well.

3

COLD GARDENS

THE PROBLEM

One of the first things that gardeners learn as they become interested in plants is that some are tougher than others. When first they see their geraniums killed by the frost this lesson begins to sink in.

There are a number of factors which control the amount of frost a plant can stand. Some plants are inherently hardier than others. This usually relates to the climate of the part of the world in which they grow naturally, so that plants from the Alps are naturally tougher than plants from Mexico. Some plants which grow naturally over a wide area may vary in their tolerance of cold, so that plants of species growing high in the mountains may be tougher than plants of the same species growing lower down. Looking a little closer at the plants, frost-hardy plants usually have a cell construction which can adapt readily to freezing and thawing, and the sugar content of the sap and the moisture in the plant cells is high so that the sap freezes less easily.

The soil in which the plant is growing can have a crucial influence. Clay and other moisture retentive soils are not usually helpful in preventing winter damage as they warm up slowly — both after a night of frost and as winter turns to spring.

Frost can cause damage not just by freezing the plant but by extracting moisture — as you will know if you put things in the refrigerator without covering them. The cold air extracts water from the foliage leaving them crisp and dry — and dead.

The site is important, too. Protection from cold winds can make a big difference as to the plants which will survive winter in a certain site. Sunshine in summer and autumn is a great help, too, as not only does this help increase the sugar content of the plant cells, so lowering their freezing point, but it also ensures that growth is ripened well before the onset of winter and so is less liable to damage. And, of course, sunshine in spring will thaw overnight frosts quickly; areas shaded in winter can sometimes remain frozen for long periods whereas other parts of the garden which get some sun thaw each day and may hardly freeze overnight.

There is some confusion between an air frost and a ground frost and how damaging each is to plants. Quite simply a ground frost occurs when the temperature drops to 32F (0C) at ground level whereas an air frost occurs when the same temperature is reached 4ft (1.2m) above ground — this is the height of a standard Stevenson Screen, the slatted white box in which meteorological equipment is usually stored.

Heat is lost from the earth's surface in winter as it radiates into the atmosphere. On cloudy or overcast nights this radiation is usually retained relatively close to the earth's surface and is absorbed by water vapour in the air. In that case temperatures at ground level do not drop too much. On clear nights, however, there is nothing to stop the heat radiating further away from the earth's surface and on such nights a radiation frost often occurs at ground level. Grassy areas are less liable to frosts caused in this way than beds of bare soil, and wet soils are less likely to suffer than dry ones.

Ground frost can be damaging to some plants, especially newly planted bedding plants in spring, and if it persists for a number of nights the ground may freeze quite deeply. This can cause a problem for some evergreens which although still losing water from their foliage cannot absorb it from the roots as the ground is frozen.

But often more damaging is an air frost. Winter and early spring flowers, such as magnolias and early cherries, can be blackened easily but air frosts are most damaging when new shoots are starting to grow, perhaps encouraged by a few unseasonably mild days. These shoots are especially vulnerable and can easily be killed.

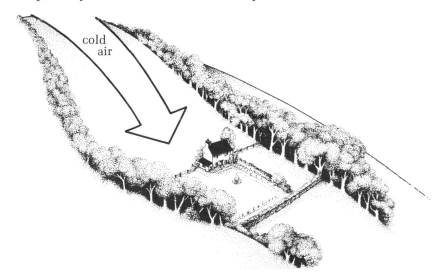

cold air

Cold air can be guided downhill by belts of trees and a hedge across its path can trap it in the garden causing a frost pocket.

Both blooms and shoots may cope with the cold, but in east facing positions the early morning sun can thaw them so quickly that the cells don't have time to adjust, and it's often at this stage that damage occurs.

There's one other way in which a frost can occur and that's when cold air drifts or is blown over the garden from elsewhere. This is where the idea of a frost pocket comes in. Cold air tends to sink and will roll downhill into hollows. It can be guided by hedges, woods and walls and these features may bring cold air towards your garden or carry it away depending on their exact location. Frosty air can build up against a hedge or wood and even something as simple as removing part of a hedge or windbreak to allow the cold air to drift through it and further downhill away from the garden can make a substantial difference.

ALLEVIATING THE PROBLEM

This is a problem where the plants do most of the work; if your climate is a harsh one there's not a great deal you can do about it, you must adapt. But you can think about the way your garden sits in the local landscape and if it seems to be in a frost pocket, see if there is a crucial hedge that could be removed or broken. It may be possible to plant a hedge on the uphill side to divert freezing air as it rolls down a gully so that most of it runs past at least part of your garden.

Within the garden, evergreens and hedges can be placed to provide

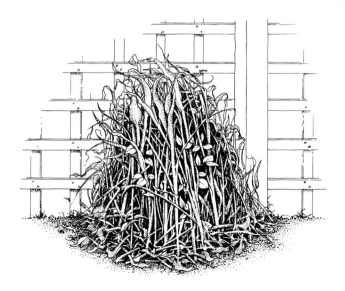

Plants at the base of a wall can be protected from frosts by covering with twigs and stems of stout grasses during the winter months.

protection from icy winds or from early morning sun and grit can be forked into the soil to enable borderline plants to benefit from improved drainage. Early-flowering shrubs with delicate blossoms should be planted against west rather than east walls so that the wall retains the last of the day's sunshine.

Plants can also be protected in more obvious ways. The roots of herbaceous plants such as eremurus can be protected by piling grit or ash over the crowns, and shrubs can be draped with sacking or plastic greenhouse shading material on especially cold nights. If plants need

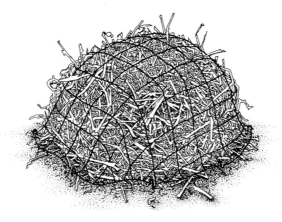

Straw, bracken, hay or other similar material can be fixed over tender perennials using netting kept in place by pegs.

Many newly planted evergreens need the protection of hessian or dense plastic netting in their first winter after planting.

protecting all winter, bracken or straw can be tied around the whole plant and left in place from late autumn until spring. Evergreens and small shrubs can also be given a little protection by erecting a screen of hessian, plastic shading or polythene set around three or four stakes and with the top left open. They can even be totally enveloped, but if you intend to cover them totally, don't use polythene as the condensation on the inside of the sheet and on the plant may freeze.

The ultimate protection, of course, is to dig the plant up and move it into a frost-free place. This is not usually possible except in the case of plants like dahlias and *Cosmos atrosanguineus* which produce tubers. But tubs, though, can be moved into a conservatory, greenhouse, garage or even a cellar where they can stay during the dormant season. If it's a dark place it must also be cool, just cool enough to keep the plant alive; plants stored in such places must not be encouraged to grow.

A variation on this is to move the plant's offspring to a frost-free place by taking cuttings in the late summer and overwintering the young plants in a frost-free greenhouse. This is a sensible precaution with any plants which are a little tender. If the parent plant survives, you will still have some valuable plants to give away or swop.

SOLVING THE PROBLEM WITH PLANTS

The choice of plants is crucial here and this can be looked at in two ways — in especially cold conditions you must choose the plants that will tolerate the harsh climate, and if you want to grow plants that are a little tender then you must help them in the ways described above.

Trees

Birch (Betula pendula) The silver birch, a familiar tree all over Europe as well as parts of Asia, is very tough indeed. It's also a very attractive tree with its white bark, slightly pendulous tips to the branches and waving habit. It thrives in most soils which are not too wet; in wet soils, *B. pubescens* is more suitable and establishes easily.

There are one or two very good forms which enhance its appeal as a small garden tree. 'Youngii' is a weeping variety which forms the most delightful spectacle when mature making a compact tree with stiffly weeping branches; it's one of the best of all small garden trees. 'Tristis' has a more pendulous habit than the common version and 'Dalecarlica' has attractive, finely cut foliage. z2

Hazel (Corylus) All the hazels are tough but one in particular makes an outstanding upright tree for medium and larger gardens. *Corylus colurna* is a tall but narrow, pyramidal tree with upswept branches and interesting corrugations on the bark. It produces yellow catkins in the spring and the autumn colour is yellow, too. z5

Serbian spruce (Picea omorika) A very attractive tree and one of my favourites, with a very unusual habit of growth. It makes a tall narrow tree with pendulous branches which then turn up sharply at the tips. The Serbian spruce is a tree which will fit into small gardens giving you the opportunity to plant a large tree that will not take up too much space. Eventually it makes a tall, slim tree and every year it becomes more attractive. z4

Whitebeam (Sorbus aria) This relative of the mountain ash, recommended for windy sites, is one of the best small trees for cold areas, although it, too, thrives in windy spots.

The foliage is very different from the divided foliage of the mountain ash, it's broad and oval with silvery undersides which show up well in a breeze. There are heads of creamy white flowers in spring, excellent autumn colour and clusters of fat red berries in autumn.

'Decaisneana' has larger than average leaves and larger fruits, while 'Lutescens' has a greyish look to the upper surface of the foliage as well as the undersides. z5

Also try... Acer platanoides, Alnus incana, Larix decidua, Picea abies, Sorbus aucuparia

Hedges

Holly (Ilex crenata) Quite different from *Ilex aquifolium*, which is more familiar in British gardens, this Japanese holly is more common in America. It's altogether a smaller plant reaching about 15ft (5m) with very small dark leaves. It makes a very good garden hedge and should usually be chosen instead of *Lonicera nitida* (z7) which tends to get floppy and bare at the base. Two good varieties for hedges are 'Convexa' with slightly convex leaves like a box and 'Golden Gem' with lovely yellowish leaves which are at their best in winter. z6

Juniper (Juniperus) Two American junipers are accommodating and tough enough to come into this category, *Juniperus scopulorum* (z4) originally from the Rocky Mountains and *J. virginiana* (z2) from eastern and central areas. They are both very hardy and, although not used as hedges in areas where other trees can be used instead, are nevertheless very suitable. Both are bluish in colour and this must be remembered when planning the garden as it's not a colour which will suit every situation.

White cedar (Thuya occidentalis) From eastern North America this tree is another really tough customer and can be used as a specimen

The cowslip is not only one of the most dainty and appealing of British wild flowers but also an excellent plant for the coldest gardens.

The new 'Galaxy' achilleas from Germany like this 'Salmon Beauty' are not only tough but also increase quickly in their first year.

tree as much as a hedge. But as a hedging plant it will thrive where the western red cedar, *Thuya plicata*, is killed by cold. The curiously named variety 'Smargd', sometimes spelt 'Smargard', is the one usually suggested as a hedge and is an especially good, bright, emerald green shade making a suitable background for flowers. z2

Also try. . . Aronia arbutifolia, Hippophae rhamnoides, Ligustrum vulgare, Prunus × cistena, Sambucus canadensis

Shrubs

Red bearberry (Arctostaphylos uva-ursi) A low, creeping shrub excellent for tumbling down rocks on the cooler sides of rock gardens. The flowers are very small and white with a hint of pink and are followed by rather more noticeable red fruits. The foliage turns an attractive dark purplish shade in winter. z4

Caragana arborescens Not brash or flamboyant, this large shrub from Siberia is a member of the pea family with long arching shoots carrying but few branches. The yellow pea flowers appear in early summer as the leaves open. There is a dwarf version, 'Nana', and a weeping form, both of which are worth growing. z2

Clematis viticella A summer-flowering species with rather slender stems making an altogether charming plant with flowers in blue or purple. Although a very tough plant the tips generally die back in winter to a strong bud but this should not alarm you. 'Abundance' is a soft mauve and 'Minuet' is creamy in colour with a large purple mark at the end of each petal; very unusual. z4

Sweet pepper bush (Clethra alnifolia) An attractive late-flowering deciduous shrub which insists on lime free soil and a constant supply of moisture; drying out is fatal. From eastern North America, this tough plant has a tendency to produce suckers, which you may or may not find useful, and doesn't usually reach more than about 7ft (2.1m). In late summer upright spikes of scented white flowers appear at the tips of the growth made earlier in the season and also at the leaf joints towards the end of the shoots. z4

Euonymus alatus If it's autumn colour you like then this shrub really will please you. It's a slow, dense growing plant with curious corky flanges on the younger stems making it most distinctive. In autumn the colour is stunning, a glorious rich red, but for the rest of the year it has to be said that this is an unremarkable shrub as the flowers and fruits are small. Bringing it to your attention has convinced me that I must make the space for one myself. z3

Kerria japonica An unusual plant grown for its stems and for its flowers. It's a large shrub, easily reaching 8ft (2.4m) high, with stout, erect, bright green shoots rising from a steadily suckering rootstock. These stems are very attractive in the winter. The flowers appear all along the branches in spring and in the variety 'Pleniflora', which is the most commonly seen, are round, densely double and about 2in (5cm) across. z4

Spiraea My favourite spiraea comes into this category and that's *Spiraea thunbergii*, one of the most attractive yet unprepossessing shrubs around. It only reaches about 6ft (1.8m) at most and is very twiggy in growth but in spring the arching branches are crowded with flat heads of pure white flowers which stand up from the shoots prettily. This is about the first of the spiraeas to flower but when it's finished its appeal is limited — but it's worth growing just for its delightful spring show. z4

Viburnum rhytidophyllum Now here's a shrub for you, a tall evergreen sometimes reaching 12ft (3.6m) with large, dark green, oval leaves on which the veins are deeply etched; the undersides are covered in fine grey felt. The flowers are disappointingly small and creamy and appear in spring but soon pass to be followed later by red fruits which turn to black. They don't fruit well but the option of providing a partner to encourage fruiting is not possible for most gardeners due to lack of space.

One intriguing habit of the plant is for the leaves to hang limp after a hard frost only to perk up again later in the day. This is a very substantial and dominating shrub owing to its size and the size of its leaves so it needs placing carefully. It's especially good on chalk soils. z5

Japanese wisteria (Wisteria floribunda) One of the classic garden plants, this twining climber is a little less vigorous than its Chinese counterpart, *W. sinensis*, usually reaching only about 12–14ft (3.6–4.2m). It can be readily distinguished from the Chinese plant by the fact that the stems twine clockwise, the Chinese plant twines the other way. The flowers are in various purplish and bluish tones.

The most astonishing variety of all is 'Macrobotrys' which carries the most extraordinarily long flower spikes, hanging down up to 3ft (90cm). Of course, this means that this variety must be planted in a suitable spot where the flowers can best be appreciated and a pergola is probably ideal.

Other varieties with less remarkable, but still very beautiful flowers include a white form ('Alba'), a pink form ('Rosea') and a double violet one ('Violacea Plena'). z4

Also try. . . Actinidia kolomikta, Cornus alba, Eleagnus commutata, Jasminum nudiflorum, Rosa rugosa

Perennials

Yarrow (Achillea) The common yarrow (*Achillea millefolium*), with its fine feathery foliage and flat heads of off-white flowers, is a weed in many gardens and one which is difficult to kill with hormone weedkillers, but even this is an attractive plant when allowed to flower. Plants with pinkish flowers are common in the wild and there are also improved cultivated versions available. 'Cerise Queen' is the only one frequently seen but a number of German varieties have recently been introduced with flowers in pink ('Appleblossom'), yellow ('Great Expectations'), pale salmon ('Salmon Beauty') and crimson ('The Beacon'). After grabbing my attention at the Chelsea Flower Show these new varieties have all grown vigorously and flowered well in their first year in the garden. z2

Ornamental onions (Allium) The ornamental onions, grown for their attractive and sometimes very large flower heads, are steadily gaining popularity and some are amongst the most hardy of all bulbs. The familiar chives (*Allium schoenoprasum*) is the one with dark, tubular leaves and round heads of pink or purplish flowers — both leaves and flowers can be used for flavouring.

Chives reaches about 12in (30cm) in height but there are two larger species which are also worth growing. At 18in (45cm) is *A. cernuum*, which the plantsman Graham Thomas describes as having flowers 'like an exploding rocket'! The flower stem turns at the top so that the head hangs down but the individual flowers counteract this by turning upwards. They are rich blue or sometimes pinkish and well worth growing.

A little taller is *A. pulchellum* with purple flowers which also behave rather strangely as they first hang down and then turn upwards as the flowers fade and the seeds develop. It's similar to the rather smaller *A. flavum*. z4

Elephant's ears (Bergenia) Big rounded foliage, which is evergreen in many varieties, and is looked upon as extremely ugly or highly attractive according to your taste. The flowers appear in spring on stems up to 18in (45cm) high and are in the range from magenta through various pinks to white. Picking good varieties is difficult but one or two stand out. *Bergenia cordifolia* 'Purpurea' (z3) is about the largest of all with foliage which turns purplish in winter and has magenta flowers in spring, but for winter foliage colour, the beetroot red *B. purpurescens* (z5) cannot be beaten. This is altogether neater in shape and colours best in a well-drained site. 'Sunningdale' is similar but is more vigorous so creating a better ground cover.

There are a number of other hybrids such as the large 'Ballawley' with rather floppy foliage and red flowers, 'Silver Light' with white flowers (both z3) which are also worth growing. As I write 'Bressingham White' is one of the most attractive plants in the garden. z3

Coreopsis verticillata This neat, upright, fine-leaved plant flowers for months from summer well into the autumn with bright yellow single daisies topping its dark foliage. It's bushy and good weed-suppressing cover but not too invasive. The most usually seen form is 'Grandiflora' which as well as being a splendid border plant is good for cutting too. New on the scene is a paler variety, 'Moonbeam', which looks to be well worth trying. z3

Globe thistle (Echinops ritro) This silvery blue globe thistle, one of the shorter growing types, reaches about 4ft (1.2m) and is the one best suited for smaller borders. It's a fine plant for a subdued but attractive late summer display especially as the colour is evident before the flowers actually open. It has a variety, *Echinops ritro* var. *tenuifolius*, which is more commonly known as *E. ruthenicus*, and is less often seen but with finely cut foliage and bright blue flowers. If something especially large and imposing is required, *E. sphaerocephalus* is the one to go for as it reaches over 6ft (1.8m) with broad foliage and large greyish flower heads. z3

Sweet rocket (Hesperis matronalis) A traditional English cottage garden favourite which although very hardy has other quirks which may prove irksome. It looks, I suppose, not unlike a huge lady's smock (*Cardamine pratensis*) growing to about 4ft (1.2m) with upright shoots topped with flowers in any shade from white to purple and every variable in between. The scent in the evening is captivating. There are double varieties, although they are so rarely seen these days that it hardly seems worth recommending them, and they must be prop-agated from cuttings regularly. The singles have a habit of becoming less productive as they age but if not dead-headed they will self-seed helpfully so providing a constant succession of young plants. z3

Musk mallow (Malva moschata) In its white form a supremely innocent looking plant. A native of the British Isles, where its usual colour is pink, it grows in pastures and hedges on the more fertile soils and in its best forms the finely cut foliage provides a splendid base for the saucer-shaped flowers which come for some weeks in summer. But the foliage can vary, so it pays to look at your plant carefully before you buy it. A lovely plant and at 3ft (90cm) suitable for any garden. Best in sun or half shade. z3

Phlox Apart from the creeping pink *Phlox adsurgens*, all are very tough indeed, but the border types are especially impressive. Best in a little shade, there's a great number of lovely forms in pinks, lilacs, blues and white making a wonderful contribution to the summer border. Recommending varieties when there are so many is not advisable as the subtlety of variation between similar varieties affects people in different ways. This also applies to scent which I cannot detect but which others tell me varies from one variety to another. So go and see some growing and smell them, too, before noting down the varieties to order. z4

Polygonum affine A highly praised plant and one with a long season of interest. Unlike some of the more tall and invasive types this is a low creeping plant, rooting as it goes, which not only covers any well-drained soil in sun well but also cascades tightly down rocks, too. The upright spikes of pink flowers appear in summer, darken to red and then turn brown in the autumn as the foliage, too, browns and stays on the plant all winter. It may only be chestnut brown but it's better than bare stems all winter. Its daintier relative, *Polygonum vaccinifolium* (z7), is less tough but more attractive. z3

Love-lies-bleeding, Amaranthus caudatus, *is a tough, easy and attractive plant but sometimes seeds itself too generously for comfort.*

Primrose (Primula) Three British species of primula all fall into this category, the primrose (*Primula vulgaris*), cowslip (*P. veris*) and oxlip (*P. elatior*). I group them together here because they are so often thought of together and because they also sometimes hybridise with each other to create intermediate forms.

The primrose, with its large flowers held singly on slender stalks, is primarily a plant of light woodland and hedgerows although in damp areas it also grows in grass. In addition to its natural pale yellow colour there is a good pale blue, 'Sibthorpii'. This is a good plant for a wild garden or to grow amongst shrubs. Many of the strains raised as pot plants are less hardy and, although they may survive outside in moist, well-drained soil in warmer areas, they could not be said to be suitable for cold gardens.

The cowslip carries a number of nodding flowers, smaller than those of the primrose, on upright stems. It's more a plant of grazed meadows and grassy areas especially on limestone where it sometimes forms large colonies. Another good wild garden plant but also good in borders. There are a number of coloured forms available from seed companies and the red and rusty shades are especially attractive.

The oxlip is altogether less common in the wild, only growing in woods on chalky clay and these are the conditions it needs to thrive in gardens. It's similar to the cowslip but the flowers are larger and paler. z3

Also try. . . Ajuga reptans, Campanula carpatica, Cimicifuga foetida, Dryas octopetala, Helleborus niger, Iris sibirica, Osmunda regalis, Pulmonaria saccharata, Tanacetum vulgare, Tiarella wherryi

Annuals and Bedding Plants

Corn cockle (Agrostemma githago) An introduced British cornfield weed that also occurs over much of Europe, the corn cockle is a tall willowy plant with slightly hairy stems and foliage, and five-petalled reddish purple flowers at the tips of the shoots. Not a dramatic plant, although its variety 'Milas' is a richer colour, but a good hardy annual for a cottage garden and to allow to self-sow amongst other plants.

Hollyhock (Althaea rosea) The problem of rust disease is such that hollyhocks should now be treated as annuals or maybe biennials as the disease persists on perennial plants and usually ends up killing them. The more dwarf varieties like 'Majorette' and 'Pinafore' can be sown outside in spring and will flower in late summer, or all types can be sown in summer to flower the following year in late spring and summer. But spraying against rust is important. The variety 'Nigra' is a tall one with deepest maroon flowers and is well worth growing in addition to the more usual shades. Best in sun.

English marigold (Calendula officinalis) Easy hardy annuals for sowing outside where they are to flower, the double flowers come at the ends of the rather sticky shoots. Varieties vary in their height from 6in (15cm) to 3ft (90cm) and in colour from lemon and apricot to deep orange and mahogany. Some especially upright varieties from Japan are particularly suitable for cut flowers. Many varieties, notably the dwarfer types, are prone to mildew so may need regular spraying.

Sweet pea (Lathyrus odorata) Tough annuals, although sowing in autumn is not to be recommended in the coldest areas. Sweet peas are available in every form from neat flat spreaders no more than 6in (15cm) high and 18in (45cm) across to tall, vigorous climbers. The taller Spencer types are the best to grow for a combination of large, freely produced flowers and strong scent.

Recommending varieties is difficult when there are so many but I suggest 'Cupid' for a really small grower, 'Jet Set' for a 3–4ft (0.9–1.2m) semi-twiner and for the traditional climbers go for 'Noel Sutton' in blue, 'Royal Wedding' in white, 'Southbourne' in pink, 'Lady Fairbairn' in lilac and 'Black Prince' in deep maroon.

Also try... Amaranthus caudatus, Atriplex hortensis 'Rubra', Chrysanthemum segetum, Ionopsidium acaule

———— 4 ————
HOT AND DRY SITES

THE PROBLEM

Anyone who has been to the Mediterranean, especially in the spring, will realise that a hot and dry site is by no means a problem if you choose the right plants. Indeed, some gardeners create dry situations in sunny places in order to grow plants that revel in these conditions.

If you look at the places where rosemary, sun roses, brooms and helichrysums grow in the wild, you will see why they are suited to hot, dry sites in the garden — they grow there naturally. The soil may be almost pure sand or gravel, possibly supplemented with a little leaf litter which burns up quickly, or it may be little more than an inch or two over solid rock, the roots penetrating through fissures and cracks. Either way the soil is poor and impoverished, the drainage is perfect and in summer there is very little moisture.

In gardens, analogous situations arise in a number of ways. You may garden on shallow soil over solid rock — in some areas chalk or limestone is often met with in this way, in others it may be something even more solid. You may find that your subsoil is pure sand or gravel and that this has found its way to the surface; this can happen after construction or road building works when, accidentally or not, the topsoil has been removed.

Such soils are dry, they burn up any organic matter that you add very quickly and there is usually a shortage of plant foods. If the substrate is rock, they can become very wet for short periods in heavy rain as the fissures cannot always cope with the amount of water that collects, but soon after they dry out and in summer are parched. Any plants requiring a steady supply of moisture are difficult to grow and vegetables are almost impossible to grow well without a great deal of effort.

ALLEVIATING THE PROBLEM

Like so many of these so called 'problems' the best way of dealing with it is to treat it as an opportunity. There is a wide range of plants that will flourish, especially if some organic matter is added to the soil, and many which will thrive without although growth may be slow.

But if you want to be less specific in the plants you grow, then further changes must be made. Increasing the amount of organic matter should be the first improvement. What you choose depends on the nature of the sand, gravel or rock that you are faced with and the plants that you wish to grow, and here testing your soil with one of the small soil test kits available in garden centres is a big help. If the test gives you a pH value of over 7 your soil is limy and if it's below 7 it's acid. The higher the figure the more limy the soil, the lower the figure the more acid. Mind you, if you look at the plants growing around you in gardens or in the lanes and hedgerows you should be able to tell if it's acid or limy but a test will convince you. Rhododendrons and blue hydrangeas are a sure sign of acid soil.

If your soil is acid, which often happens in sandy soils, and you want to grow acid loving plants, then moss peat is the most convenient form of organic matter to add to maintain the acidity. Leaf mould is another option but don't get it from areas on different soils as the leaf mould from, for example, beech trees growing on chalk, is far more limy than that from birch trees growing on sand. Garden compost from your own garden is another alternative.

Forking organic matter into the upper layer of hot, dry soils helps them retain the moisture they need to grow a wider range of plants.

If your soil is only slightly acid and you would like to make it even less so, spent mushroom compost may be the best choice. Because it contains gypsum and has a naturally high pH it makes soils more alkaline. So it can help bring slightly acid soils nearer to the neutral figure of pH7 or even slightly above.

Whichever material you use, you'll need plenty of it. There's so much air in these open soils that organic matter decays very quickly and needs adding regularly. Fortunately, both peat and spent mushroom compost are available in bulk which is a great deal more economical than buying large quantities of silly little bags.

Because these soils are well-drained, plant foods leach out very quickly and these too may need adding regularly. Most of the plants I am going to suggest will not thrive on lavish feeding and thorough preparation of the planting hole is usually enough. A light dressing of bonemeal every spring is helpful on limy soils after a few years (wear gloves as it dries the skin very badly) or, if you aspire to something richer and want to grow a broader range of plants, a regular mulch plus a balanced general fertiliser such as John Innes Base is probably better.

On acid soils, where the peat releases few nutrients as it breaks down, En-Mag is an excellent fertiliser both for specific acid lovers and more general plantings.

As well as alleviating the problems of drought and the lack of plant foods, there's also the problem of the heat to contend with. This can be solved in the long term and short term in different ways.

In the short term, new plantings may need to be protected from the sun by shade netting and this can be especially necessary for conifers and other evergreens. Shading from sun will reduce the amount of water being lost from the foliage before the roots have had a chance to establish themselves.

In the longer term, shade can be supplied by fences or trees. A fence or wall can transform an area in no time, its dense shade reducing water loss hugely but it will also bring a change to the type of plants that will thrive. The thin shade of carefully chosen trees — even just one or two specimens — is often preferable, though they should be positioned to give a little respite rather than to change the character of the area. They will also provide valuable shelter from cold winds which many of the plants best suited to growing on relatively unimproved sites of this type will appreciate.

On acid soils, conifers like *Cupressus glabra* (z7) and its various forms are good in this respect as are junipers and pines while on soils with a higher pH, yews, *Thuya occidentalis* (z2) and *T. plicata* (z5) in their various forms, are better choices. Don't plant them as long screens unless they only cast shade for part of the day but rather as specimens to cast a passing shade as the sun goes round.

SOLVING THE PROBLEM WITH PLANTS

One thing worth remembering about this sort of site is that plants with silvery foliage are amongst the most likely to thrive. The silvery coating has evolved to prevent the leaves losing too much moisture and plants with this feature thrive naturally in hot, dry conditions. Many will rot in shadier, richer, or more moist sites.

Trees

Field maple (Acer campestre) This is a British native tree found on alkaline soils and doesn't cast too dense a shade so it's a good tree if you intend to plant shade lovers. It's a round-headed tree, the young growth is sometimes tinged with pink and in the autumn the colours are especially long lasting in golds and reds. It sometimes branches very low down so the occasional limb may need removing. z5

Incense cedar (Calocedrus decurrens) Growing wild in the south western United States from Oregon to southern California but often seen elsewhere, this tree has a very distinctive columnar shape. It makes a large tree growing on average about 12in (30cm) a year. Its shape is unmistakable — very narrow with parallel sides and a flat top; the foliage is dark green. Think of it as a hardier version of the Italian cypress so often seen in the Mediterranean. In the worst soils it can lose its lower foliage but the degree of cultivation around it will usually ensure that it thrives. z6

Mount Etna broom (Genista aetnensis) Sometimes more of a large, sparse shrub than a tree but it can be encouraged into tree-like growth in the early stages by not allowing too much branching. It usually reaches about 20ft (6m) although there is a larger tree in a garden near Kew Gardens in London. This tree is unusual in having almost no leaves at all and the bright golden, scented flowers appear in large numbers on virtually bare branches in July. The branches are thin and wiry, casting very little shade. An unusual tree but one which is not difficult to grow. z8

Honey locust (Gleditsia triacanthos) A large tree with an open crown, this is one of the latest trees to break into leaf and so gives smaller plants time to make the best of the spring sun. It thrives in dry soils and those with few nutrients and tolerates pollution well too; a real tough customer.

It's also tough in another sense for the whole tree is covered in spines which can inflict a nasty wound. There is a variety, 'Inermis', which is without spines and there is also a very attractive slower growing variety, 'Sunburst'. The young foliage of 'Sunburst' is bright yellow and it steadily fades to pale green through the season. One more variety worth considering is the American 'Ruby Lace' which makes an even smaller tree, and has young growth of ruby red which fades to green with a strong bronze tint. z5

Also try. . . Robinia pseudacacia, Juniperus communis 'Hibernica'

Hedges

Lavender (Lavandula) Good as specimen shrubs as well as informal hedges, quite a number of varieties is available and all make good low hedges – choose your variety according to the height you need and the foliage and flower colour you prefer. 'Hidcote' (z7) is the best known and is neat in growth, modest in height, 2–2½ft (60–75cm), with grey green foliage and violet flower spikes. 'Hidcote Giant' (z7) is altogether larger, with paler flowers and broader foliage; 'Munstead' (z7) is similar in height to 'Hidcote' but with greener foliage and blue flowers.

I like 'Vera' (z7), the Dutch lavender, which reaches 4ft (1.2m) with broad grey foliage and lavender flowers and also *L. stoechas* (z8), the French lavender, which is another dwarf type with very dark, purple flowers in dense heads.

Attention from shears is needed after flowering to keep them neat — and don't be too timid.

Catmints and red valerian, an attractive summer combination of easy plants for hotter sites where moisture is in short supply.

Western red cedar (Thuya plicata) A very tolerant plant which does well in these situations if you need a formal hedge. Appropriate varieties also make good specimen trees. The variety to choose for hedging is 'Atrovirens' with bright, glossy leaves which make a good background to other plants; it only needs cutting once a year in late summer. Think carefully before planting a formal hedge of this type as the roots will take a substantial amount of water from the soil and this may not suit the type of gardening in which you intend to indulge. z5

Also try. . . Coronilla glauca, Olearia × scillonensis

Shrubs

Sun rose (Cistus) Generally reckoned to be rather tender, on gravelly and stony soils in full sun it's much tougher. Although the flowers only last for a day, or less, they appear in such numbers that the display is never thin. Even when they have finished flowering the evergreen foliage is usually attractive. *C. ladanifer*, with huge ruffled white flowers, each with a purple mark at the base and dark narrow leaves, is one of the hardiest and one of the largest, too, reaching 6ft (1.8m). *C. salvifolius* is similar though smaller and with a yellow basal mark. 'Silver Pink' with silvery foliage and pink flowers is also hardy and *C. × purpureus* has pink flowers with a dark base and sage-like foliage; it needs the poorest soil to thrive. z8

Convolvulus cneorum The white silky hairs on the evergreen foliage make this shrub attractive all the year round, and the appearance of soft pink flowers in May completes the picture delightfully. Although related to a number of ghastly rampageous weeds this is a well behaved shrub rarely reaching more than 2ft (60cm) in height and making a neat though not unpleasantly bun-shaped bush if pruned hard when young. If left unpruned it can develop rather floppy growth. Containerised plants grown in a peat-based compost are less likely to survive wet, cold winters than those grown in a traditional soil-based compost with good drainage. z8

Broom (Cytisus) Varying in size from the Mount Etna broom mentioned earlier to *C. ardoinii* (z7), a neat little mat former. *C. battandieri* (z7) makes a substantial shrub, good on walls, but also in the open on gravelly soil. It has greyish foliage and large clusters of yellow flowers which are said to smell of honey or pineapple! It flowers in July.

Many of the common hybrid brooms that come in such a variety of colours are short-lived on the poorest soils but are still worth growing if you've managed to improve them. The creamy 'C. E. Pearson' (z7) is especially appealing. The smaller types, such as *C. × beanii* (z6) with brilliant yellow flowers and *C. × kewensis* (z6) with creamy flowers, only reach about 12–15in (30–38cm) while *C. ardoinii* (z7) is just a green mat of stems and tiny leaves with bright yellow flowers in spring.

Helichrysum A huge group of plants which includes shrubs, border perennials, alpines and annuals, there are some excellent shrubs amongst them, many with silvery leaves. *H. splendidum* (z9) is a stiff upright plant at first with silvery grey foliage and yellow everlasting flowers in summer which keep their colour for months. It's best pruned each spring to keep it neat. *H. serotinum* (z8), also known as *H. angustifolium*, is known as the curry plant from the distinctive smell of the crushed leaves which are long, narrow and silvery. Finally, making a rather larger plant at 3ft (90cm) high and as much wide is *H. fontanesii* (z8). The leaves are long and narrow with a heavy white felt and clusters of yellow flowers in summer. One of my favourites.

Rosemary (Rosmarinus officinalis) Wonderful plants with a powerful scent to the foliage and blue flowers starting in spring but often appearing over long periods. They come in upright types, like the indispensable 'Miss Jessop' (z6), which also makes a good hedge, spreading types like 'Suffolk Blue' (z6) and arching ones like 'Seven Seas' (z6).

My own favourite is *R. lavandulaceus* (z9) with its darker, shorter leaves and spreading habit which makes a very elegant plant trailing over a rock. There are many more but most have the same blue flowers — except for the pink-flowered 'Majorca' (z6) and 'Roseus' (z6), neither of which is often seen and a rare white. There is an equally rare variety with golden splashed leaves.

I find that a combined thin and trim after the main flowering keeps the taller types from getting too straggly and keeps the bushier ones dense. I always agonise about whether to leave the snow on the branches to protect the shoots from frost, or knock it off to prevent the weight breaking the fragile branches. The latter usually wins but this year my *R. lavandulaceus* has suffered badly.

Sage (Salvia) There are far more salvias than the familiar red bedding plants. Altogether there are many hundreds and they cover shrubs, perennials, annuals and biennials but the culinary sage, *Salvia officinalis* (z6), must be one of the best for hot, dry situations. The plants are spreading with very attractive foliage and even the ordinary culinary sage with its grey green leaves is an appealing plant. There are other varieties, too; 'Purpurescens' has purple foliage, 'Icterina' has soft gold variegations and 'Tricolor' has its leaves splashed with pink and cream and makes an especially neat plant — although a slightly less robust one.

They all benefit hugely from a trim and tidy in spring and can suffer in the coldest weather, though in sunny sites and well-drained soil this is less common.

There are a number of more tender species such as the pineapple sage, *Salvia rutilans* (z9), with loose spikes of magenta flowers very late in the season and *S. microphylla var. neurepia* (z8) with scarlet flowers on open bushes about 4ft (1.2m) high. It pays to take cuttings of these varieties and overwinter them in a frost-free place, just in case.

Teurium fruticans A fine vigorous grey-leaved shrub usually grown against a south wall but also surviving in the open in a hot, sunny, well-drained spot. The flowers are blue and last for some months and the rather angular branching is interesting. The growth can be straggly and occasional heavy pruning may be necessary to keep it in order. Do this in spring, although it will delay flowering. There is a good specimen on the wall of the pub near Margery Fish's wonderful garden at East Lambrook in Somerset. z8

Yucca Big rosettes of spine-tipped foliage and upright spikes, densely clustered in white bells. Wonderful. There are a number of species from the southern United States and further south, so many of them are rather tender. I like *Yucca whipplei* (z9) with its neat rosettes of narrow grey foliage and dramatic flowers, but not only is it difficult to find, it's also not reliably hardy. So instead try *Y. filamentosa* (z5), so called because the leaves shed fine silvery threads. It's another neat species but a hardy one which, unlike some, produces its masses of creamy flowers when quite young. *Y. gloriosa* (z6) is altogether more massive, eventually forming a short stout trunk and taking some years to flower — but when it does the spikes can be 6ft (1.8m) high.

Also try. . . Mutisia ilicifolia, Perovskia atriplicifolia, Phlomis fruti-cosa, Ruta graveolens, Spartium junceum

Perennials

Alstroemeria Don't grow only the old orange horror that rampages everywhere without a thought for more choice plants — there are others. They are all relatively restrained in dry soil and need the sun to flourish. Plant them out from small pots as they resent too much disturbance and are sometimes difficult to divide. The 'Ligtu Hybrids' are the most widely seen, in shades of pink, coral, salmon and orange but the newer 'Princess Lilies' from Holland, all named after princesses, flower longer and more prolifically in a wider range of shades though I have not yet tried them on poor soil. z7

Spurge (Euphorbia) Many are suitable but I will pick just two, in contrasting styles. *E. myrsinites* (z6) is a flat ground hugger falling over small rocks or laying across a stone. The leaves are bluish grey while the flowers at the ends of the 1ft (30cm) long shoots are pale olive. Very pretty and unusual. *E. characias* (z7) is quite different. A tall upright plant usually reaching 4ft (1.2m) once established, and often more, with dusky grey green leaves darkening in the winter and topped in spring with fat heads of olive flowers, each with a maroon eye. A majestic plant at its best. Its close relation, *E. wulfenii* (z7), has paler flowers without the maroon eye. A second relation is the excellent *E. × martinii* (z7) which is altogether smaller and more compact with reddish stems and foliage.

Summer hyacinth (Galtonia candicans) A wonderful summer-flowering bulb with open spires of scented white flowers hanging down prettily. It reaches 4ft (1.2m) and looks wonderful emerging from amongst other plants. In my garden it casts its seed about liberally and new plants are always appearing but on poor soil a few liquid feeds during the growing season, tomato food is fine, will also encourage its bulbs to divide prolifically. z7

Perennial candytuft (Iberis sempervirens) One of the most familiar of rock plants making flat spreading plants, 9–12in (23–30cm) high, so densely covered in white flowers in spring that the foliage is almost totally hidden. *Iberis sempervirens* (z4) is altogether an easy and reliable, lovely and accommodating plant. There is a slightly smaller version with lilac flushed flowers called *Iberis gibraltarica* (z8). *I. semperflorens* (z8) is more stiff and upright reaching about 2ft (60cm) in mild seasons and flowers for most of the year, though in bad winters

Houseleeks like this 'Rubine' survive in hot sites with almost no water and can even grow happily with a roothold amongst roof tiles.

it may succumb to frost. A rather sparsely clothed plant in many cases but valuable for its late flowers.

Raoulia Sometimes known as the vegetable sheep from the way that in its wild home in New Zealand some species form huge dense rounded clumps. *R. australis* is the usual one grown in the UK and it makes ground hugging carpets, little more than 1in (2.5cm) high, made up of tiny silvered rosettes which spread densely over the surface of the soil. *R. tenuicaulis* is similar but less grey and will put up with the foliage from under-planted bulbs, like crocuses, flopping on to it. z7

Houseleek (Sempervivum) You can tell that houseleeks are a good choice for this situation as they grow superbly on south facing tiled roofs, with no more roothold than the cracks between the tiles. They used to be planted there as a protection against lightning. Houseleeks thrive in gravel and sunshine, the red-leaved varieties producing especially colourful rosettes. The rosettes make dense clusters,

Grey foliage plants like this Senecio leucostachys *are amongst the best choices for hot, dry sites as well as stony and gravelly soils.*

spreading slowly, and in spring the heads of pink, yellow or occasionally white flowers are pretty, too. 'Rubine' is an excellent red-leaved variety, 'Commander Hay' has broad green leaves with red marks while S. *arachnoideum* produces white webbing amongst its rounded rosettes. z5

Tulip (Tulipa) Another bulb ideally suited to this situation as it needs a good baking in the summer months to ripen the bulbs well. This leads to more prolific flowering the following season. Tulips need feeding, too; cut the dead flowers off as soon as they fade, unless you want to gamble on some self-sown seedlings, then feed every two weeks with a liquid feed until the leaves die off.

Those best suited to this treatment are species and the smaller varieties. The 6in (15cm) 'Franz Lehar' with a pale yellow flower over prettily marked leaves is good but better is 'Red Riding Hood', a little taller with scarlet flowers over purple striped foliage. There are many more, look out for those in the *fosteriana*, *greigii* and *kaufmanniana* groups. Other species such as T. *tarda* in yellow and white, T. *linifolia* in scarlet with a dark centre and T. *urumiensis* in deep gold with the petals backed with bronze are amongst the many worth trying. z5

Californian fuchsia (Zauschneria) An unusual rock plant in flowering in late summer and autumn when many others are past their best. Z. *californica* makes a bushy plant about 12–18in (30–45cm) high and the variety 'Glasnevin' with a dense growth of downy, greyish foliage shows off the tubular scarlet flowers especially well. It starts to flower in late summer and continues well into the autumn. z8

Also try. . . Allium species, Anthemis cupaniana, Cynara scolymus, Nerine bowdenii, Osteospermum species

Annuals and Bedding Plants

Rock purslane (Calandrinia) Startling magenta flowers, with a noticeable sheen, on small plants no more than 6in (15cm) high. They should be raised in a little warmth at first and need care in the early stages or damping off may strike the seedlings down, so use a well-drained compost and don't over water. The colour of the flowers means that neighbouring plants need to be selected with care to avoid an unpleasant clash of colours.

Californian poppy (Eschscholtzia) Brilliant sun lovers which self-seed happily all over the place. Most are varieties of E. *californica* which reaches about 12in (30cm) with such names as 'Cherry Ripe', 'Orange King' and 'Milky-White' conveniently identifying the different shades. The mixtures are rather variable, some include purple shades, others do not and if you let them self-sow without interference you end up with mostly orange. Another species, *E. caespitosa*, is a little shorter with small yellow flowers. Very pretty.

Mexican tulip poppy (Hunnemannia fumariifolia) Like the Californian poppy this is a member of the poppy family but is much taller, reaching 2–3ft (60–90cm) with big flowers at about 3in (7.5cm) across. It's less hardy, too, and can be raised in a little heat at first though is best pricked out into individual pots to avoid the root disturbance which it dislikes so much. 'Sunlite' is a variety which is sometimes seen and this grows a little shorter.

Livingstone daisy (Mesembryanthemum) Succulent annuals with bright flowers, each with many fine petals. Two types are usually found. There is a mixture of magenta, pink, orange and whitish shades which comes under such names as 'Magic Carpet Mixed', and a lovely compact yellow called 'Yellow Ice' which is also known as 'Lunette'. 'Yellow Ice' in particular has its flowering season greatly prolonged if the dead flowers are removed.

Portulaca In the UK they are at their best in really hot summers as some varieties close their flowers in dull weather. In California they are much more popular. They make creeping plants whose succulent foliage covers banks well. The flowers come in shining magenta, yellow, red, various pinks and white and can be double or semi-double according to the variety. Another to be raised in warmth in all but the most favoured areas. Water thoughtfully in the seedling stages as rotting off is common.

Also try. . . Gazania varieties, *Lupinus* varieties, *Zinnia* varieties

5

SEASIDE GARDENS

THE PROBLEM

Gardening by the sea shares a number of similarities with gardening in windy areas — with the added hazards of wind-blown salt and sand but the bonus of a warmer climate. The problems of gardening in windy areas and in windy gardens are described in detail in Chapter 1 but, although most of the comment is relevant, not all the plants that are described will also thrive in the face of a salty wind.

The warmth, of course, can hardly be described as a problem as it enables a far wider range of plants to be grown than in gardens only a few miles away inland. Plants grown in coastal gardens will be happy many hundreds of miles further north than is usual for a similar garden inland. The reason for this especially equable climate is, of course, the proximity of the sea. This works in two ways.

First, the very presence of so much water has a noticeable effect. It cools down less quickly than the land in autumn and so during the winter continues to have a warming effect on coastal areas. In the spring everything starts off a little warmer than inland so the edge is taken off the frost that little bit sooner. Therefore the overall influence is a benign one, softening the effects of winter and hastening the onset of spring. Second, warm sea currents can help keep winter temperatures from dropping as low as inland areas.

If you live in a seaside area you'll soon be aware of the situation on your coast. The climate on the west coast of England, Wales, Scotland and Ireland is greatly improved by the balmy influence of the North Atlantic Drift which enables tender plants to be grown at latitudes which would seem to prevent their growth. Gardens like Inverewe and Logan on the west coast of Scotland are testament to this and in Devon and Cornwall, which are surrounded by sea, there are many examples of gardens which can grow very tender plants; some of these gardens rarely get a frost at all. The Scilly Isles, right out in the path of the

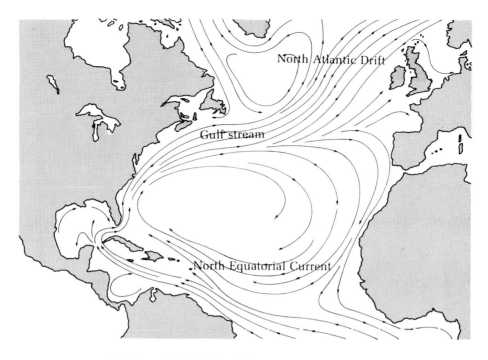

The beneficial effects of the warm ocean currents.

North Atlantic Drift, are perhaps the best example. The Florida Peninsula also shows the benefits of its position.

This warmth sometimes leads to curious happenings. I remember seeing a garden just a short walk from the sea near Malahide Castle, on the east coast of Ireland, with petunias and wallflowers flowering together merrily.

If there was only wind and warmth to contend with there would be no need of special plantings but, unfortunately, there is also the salt. This comes in the wind and the rain and has an intensely desiccating effect which damages the shoots, foliage and flowers of many seemingly tough plants. Sometimes it can even be seen as crystals on the foliage and on walls and paving where the water has evaporated. Salt has a tendency to draw water from anything with which it comes into contact and only plants which are resistant to this will thrive.

ALLEVIATING THE PROBLEM

This is mainly a matter of protecting plants from salt-laden winds, so shelter is paramount. Unless you move from your seaside garden you're stuck with the problem and, unlike most of the other difficulties described in this book, there is little you can do about it. It's something you have to live with and which will always influence

Even newly planted shelterbelts may need hessian or plastic windbreak protection from strong, salty winds in their first season.

your gardening and the plants you grow: of course, it will also make your garden distinctive and special.

So, a chapter on alleviating the problem has relatively little to say except on the subject of shelter — the rest is in the planting and the better the shelter, the wider the range of planting possible.

Planting shelter should be almost the first thing you do after the furniture is off the lorry. Now you may have bought your particular house because of its sea view and by protecting the garden with trees the view may eventually be obliterated. Well, this is a dilemma you will just have to think about; the conclusion you come to will be your own. There are plants which will thrive without any shelter and you may have to stick to them. But even if you don't plant shelter for the garden as a whole you will need it for sitting out areas at least.

Some of the trees, shrubs and shelter plants recommended for windy areas and windy gardens are also ideal for seaside planting and these are mentioned later but they may all need protecting from the salt in their early stages. Plastic windbreak material is ideal for this and although not the most elegant addition to the garden it will nevertheless do a good job. For gardeners a little more concerned with the look of the garden, even at this early stage, wattle hurdles are also suitable. Individual plants can be protected by shields of polythene.

Although walls have their disadvantages in providing shelter, within a garden they can be more useful than as a boundary. This is because you can plant in such a way that the turbulence that the walls tend to create is all but eliminated and this is what I would suggest in seaside areas. A wall and attendant planting can create an area of absolute calm and in spring and autumn as well as in summer this can be very valuable. Some of the trees listed in the chapter on wind will do a good job. But even these need temporary shelter while they get used to their new home and wattle fencing or, especially, plastic windbreak netting is ideal material to do the job.

SOLVING THE PROBLEM WITH PLANTS

Trees

Monterey cypress (Cupressus macrocarpa) A fast growing tree which in colder areas is a little delicate when young, but which makes a fine specimen tree for coastal planting being both elegant and good shelter. It becomes a large tree with dense foliage and is altogether an excellent choice, especially as it's an attractive tree when quite small. There are a number of yellow-leaved varieties; 'Goldcrest' is my favourite and it colours better in a little shade. There are many others in a good range of different forms, weeping, broadly spreading, conical and dwarf types, too. By choosing different varieties, plants of various sizes, habits and colours can be grown, and all are very tolerant of salty winds. z7

Corsican pine (Pinus nigra maritima) A tough little pine for any soil and in spite of coming from southern Europe tolerant of much colder areas. Although not especially attractive, it's invaluable for shelter and needs little protection, although it will benefit from shelter in the early stages. Eventually reaching quite a large size, if used as shelter it needs underplanting as the lower branches tend to fall away. z4

Holm oak (Quercus ilex) A large stately evergreen making a substantial tree of pleasing, rounded shape with glossy leathery foliage which is often slightly grey underneath. Although not happy in the very coldest areas this is otherwise a supremely tolerant tree putting up with shade, most soils except very heavy ones and it can also be clipped into a hedge. One interesting feature of the tree is its great variety of leaf shape and size, many variants being found on the same tree. z7

Also try. . . Acer pseudoplatanus, Populus alba, Prunus padus

Hedges

Tree purslane (Atriplex halimus) A vigorous, silvery-leaved shrub ideal for creating an informal hedge, the tree purslane can stand in the first line of defence against the salty blast and will still retain some foliage in winter. In the UK it rarely seems to flower and although sometimes tipped back by unusually hard frosts, it soon more than makes up for its loss. z8

Escallonia Always cited as a good seaside plant and quite justifiably so. As a hedge it is ideal — evergreen, flowering well, tolerating clipping and also tolerating a vicious cutting back if it gets too large or spreading. 'C. F. Ball' with crimson flowers is one of the best, 'Crimson Spire' is more upright in habit if you prefer a slightly more formal look, 'Ingramii' is pink. For more of a windbreak than a hedge try *Escallonia punctata* which is altogether taller with larger leaves and crimson flowers. z7

Fuchsia There is one splendid variety which makes excellent hedges and is often seen in Ireland and south west England. 'Riccartonii' is the one used and can make a substantial barrier in any area. The flowers are of typical fuchsia shape and archetypal colour although small. The soil needs to be well-drained and any situation suits it except full shade. The birds seem to like the hedge for shelter and nesting. z7

Also try. . . × Cupressocyparis leylandii, Griselinia littoralis, Rosmarinus officinalis

Shrubs

Euonymus japonicus A large-leaved evergreen growing to a substantial size with dark glossy foliage. The plain green form is not often cultivated but there are a number of variegated forms which make excellent plants for the back of the mixed border. 'Aureopictus' has a big golden blotch in the middle of each leaf, 'Ovatus Aureus' has a more irregular creamy patterning but best of all I like 'Macrophyllus Albus' with its broad white edging to the leaves making it very distinctive and showy.

There is a small group of quite different varieties which are dwarf in habit and with very small foliage. 'Microphyllus' is plain green with leaves about the size of box while 'Microphyllus Variegatus' is an improvement with a white edge to the foliage. z8

Griselinia Not for cold areas, this cheery evergreen, usually with an upright habit, is another standard for maritime gardens and none the worse for that. *Griselinia littoralis* is the only one ever seen in garden centres and gardens and this is a bright evergreen making a substantial shrub in mild areas but which can be cut back in cold spots elsewhere. Any type of soil seems to suit it although poor infertile sites will not bring out its good qualities. There are two variegated forms, 'Dixon's Cream' has irregular markings and the rather more common 'Variegata' has leaves with striking white marks. Good as a hedge as well as a shrub. z8

Shrubby veronica (Hebe) A number of varieties are suitable in the slightly milder than usual climate near the sea and tolerate the less advantageous facets of coastal life. *Hebe brachysiphon* (z8) makes a rounded bush with small dark foliage and stubby spikes of white flowers, while rather larger in every way is *Hebe salicifolia* (z7). The leaves are willow-like and fresh green in colour and there are long spikes of lilac flowers into the bargain. A splendid plant combining beauty and the provision of shelter.

The third in this trio is *Hebe speciosa* (z9) or rather the large number of hybrids that have been derived from it. These are excellent plants and come in a variety of purples and lilacs, many with at least a flush of purple in the leaves. 'Alicia Amherst' is deep purple, 'La Seduisante' is purplish crimson, 'Simon Delaux' is crimson.

Sea buckthorn (Hippophae rhamnoides) A versatile British plant well worth growing in all gardens and not just those near the coast. It makes a tall shrub, though not a dense one, with long, narrow silver foliage. In the autumn there are brilliant orange berries, often densely packed on the branches, which usually stay on the bushes for most of the winter and slowly turn yellow in spring. As with hollies, the fruits are carried only on female plants so both males and females should be planted. Any soil suits them as long as it's not too wet, and they're best in the sun. z3

Daisy bush (Olearia) These New Zealand shrubs are amongst the best of all for coastal conditions, shrugging off the desiccating wind easily. They are all evergreen and have small, white, daisy-like flowers and thrive in the sun. *Olearia macrodonta* (z8) is one of the best with wavy, holly-like foliage of a slightly greyish green, more intensely silvery underneath. The loose spikes of white flowers are scented and appear in early summer. This makes a good shelter plant reaching 10ft (3m) and providing well filtered protection as well as forming a striking specimen. *Olearia* × *haasti* (z7) is altogether smaller and a little slower growing with small leaves and white flowers in summer. It makes an especially good hedge. Finally *O.* × *scilloniensis* (z8) which is smaller again and neater, too, with the familiar white flowers covering the plant well.

Senecio There has been some confusion about this plant. Until recently *Senecio greyi* was the name always known for this large, straggly, grey-leaved shrub with its masses of yellow daisy flowers in summer. However, this plant has now been shown to be a hybrid and is known as 'Sunshine' and under this name it's now being more frequently listed. Its tendency to legginess and untidiness can be cured with judicial pruning each spring.

Much less commonly seen is *S. monroi* which grows into an altogether smaller plant with wavy leaves and yellow flowers. Both are at their best on a well-drained soil and in full sun.

One other which I've not seen but which is heartily recommended for seaside gardens is *Senecio reinoldii*. A medium-sized shrub with such dense growth that it filters the wind very efficiently, it has rather insignificant flowers and large leathery leaves. It's said to 'take the full blast of the Atlantic Ocean' and you can't ask much more than that. z8

Tamarisk (Tamarix) Tall, rather straggly shrubs much improved by regular pruning, the tamarisks have long willowy branches, fine feathery foliage and plumes of tiny pink flowers. They thrive in most soils except shallow, chalky ones. *Tamarix pentandra* can sometimes make a small tree with attractive dark red branches, slightly bluish leaves and large plumes of pink flowers at the ends of the shoots in summer. A lovely plant which greatly benefits from fairly hard pruning in the spring.

Although thriving in coastal gardens this is not a plant to take the full brunt of the salt-laden winds. *T. tetrandra* has much darker foliage, flowers earlier and is best pruned after flowering; *T. gallica*, which originally came from south Europe, is happy on the British coast and has become naturalised. Originally planted to stabilise shingle it has stood the exposure of such situations so well that it has spread away from its original sites. Pale pink flowers in long narrow spikes in summer. z5

Also try. . . Eleagnus ebbingei, Lonicera periclymenum, Ribes sanguineum, Rosa pimpinellifolia

Perennials

Thrift (Armeria) If the idea of following a plant's natural inclinations when deciding how to cultivate it is observed closely, we immediately arrive at thrift as the ideal seaside plant. For it's quite likely that just over the seaside garden fence it will be growing on rocky ledges of short turf, its rounded heads of pink flowers on short but strong stems waving in the sea breeze.

Thrift is a cushion-forming plant with long narrow dark green leaves overlapping to form a steadily spreading, often slightly undulating, mat. It grows in any well-drained soil in the sun and the flower heads are usually not more than 9in (23cm) high. They come in various pinks, some dark like 'Bloodstone' and 'Dusseldorf Pride', others much paler like 'Birch Pink'. z3

Catananche caerulea Such a delicate blue it seems a pity to expose the flowers to such a hammering, and indeed they will suffer if so treated, but behind shelter they are good. Reaching about 2ft (60cm) the flowers appear all summer and are a soft, slightly lilac blue with darker centre. Although the flowers are lovely the narrow foliage is rather sparse so put them closely amongst other plants. These are short-lived plants and need increasing from root cuttings every few years. z4

Seakale (Crambe) The edible seakale, *Crambe maritima*, doesn't usually stray outside the vegetable garden except by accident but it's worth growing for its broad sea green foliage and, as it grows naturally on sea shingle and sand, you can expect it to be at home in coastal gardens. In late spring there are large heads of small white flowers reaching about 2ft (60cm).

A much larger version more often cultivated in gardens is *C. cordifolia* — and this really is large. When in flower it reaches 6ft (1.8m) or more, with a huge cloud of small white flowers on long stems which will need staking discreetly with a bamboo cane to each stem. The foliage sets off the flowers well being very dark green and rather droopy. Definitely not for the front line but worth considering if your garden is a large one. z7

Lyme grass (Elymus arenarius) An excellent grey-leaved grass which grows naturally on sand dunes — so that tells you the conditions it prefers. It can reach up to 4ft (1.2m) in the rather more fertile conditions of a garden but is extremely invasive and must be planted only after careful thought as to the consequences. The spikes of flowers are bluish, too, and the effect of large clumps is delightful — if only it were better behaved I could recommend it for every garden. z4

Spurge (Euphorbia characias) A substantial perennial needing a well-drained soil and that little extra warmth that coastal regions automatically provide to ensure that it comes through the winter easily. It makes a large plant 4ft (1.2m) high made up of stout slightly reddish stems with narrow grey green leaves and topped in early spring with large heads of pale olive-coloured flowers, each with a maroon eye. *Euphorbia wulfenii* is paler in colour and without the dark eye. Don't be alarmed when the stems die after flowering, this is no more than natural behaviour. Not for the front line but wonderful architectural plants. z7

Red hot poker (Kniphofia) Not all red hot pokers are coarse and orange, I'm glad to say there are many excellent varieties which will grow very close to the sea and some have become naturalised along the shoreline — always a sign of a contented plant. There's a huge number of varieties, some a little tender in inland areas but usually happy on the coast, and they range in colour from orange through yellow to cream and in size from 4ft (1.2m) to 2ft (60cm).

'Little Maid' is at the short end of the range with flowers of the palest primrose while at the other end of the height scale there is 'Atlanta', not named after the Georgian state capital, but after a hotel in Cornwall

Wallflowers are often seen growing
naturally near the sea.

Flowering currants make huge early-
flowering shrubs in seaside areas.

Osteospermums overwinter happily – and flower for months – in seaside areas
when they might be killed by frost a few miles further inland.

where the original plant was found. This plant has orange flowers in generous numbers and has naturalised itself in many places along the British coast, sometimes even when it is splashed by spray. There are many more; I suggest you see them growing and choose exactly the shade you like. z6

African daisy (Osteospermum) Sometimes known as *Dimorphotheca*, these slightly woody plants are on the borderline of tenderness in some areas but near the sea the extra mildness usually means they overwinter happily without damage. They are upright or rather sprawling plants which, although technically shrubs owing to the woody stems near ground level, are usually listed amongst the perennials instead, as the tops are often knocked back by frost. The flowers are large daisies in many colours.

This is a group where there have been many new introductions in recent years. Of the more prostrate growing types I like *D. ecklonis* 'Prostrata' which is white with a blue disc and self-explanatory 'Tresco Purple' and 'Tresco Pink'. Amongst the more upright types 'Buttermilk' is creamy beige; 'Whirligig' is blue and white and looks rather like a single, spider flowered chrysanth; 'Pink Whirls' is a pink version. There are many more, I've yet to come across a poor one. z8

New Zealand flax (Phormium tenax) Twenty years ago these were hardly grown except in milder areas but now with the arrival of new varieties from New Zealand they are more popular, though still at their best in mild coastal areas. Basically they look like huge flag irises and it's mainly for their foliage that they are grown. They do flower, with reddish flowers on stout stems. The various forms all have different coloured and marked leaves and vary in height from 2–6½ft (0.6–2m).

'Purpureum' is about the biggest with broad, stiff purple foliage and 'Variegatum' is almost as large with yellow leaves. Half the size are 'Cream Delight' with a creamy centre to the leaf and a green edge and 'Sundowner' with a creamy pink edge and greyish purple central stripe. At the lower end of the height range is 'Yellow Wave' with golden leaves margined in green. They're not cheap as they multiply slowly but if you like exotic foliage get them all. z7

Senecio pulcher A useful plant in that it flowers very late in the season and its daisy-like flowers are an unusual shade of magenta with a yellow disc. The plant only reaches about 18in (45cm) in height and has rather leathery foliage, and it needs well-drained soil in the sunshine as well as the mildness that coastal conditions provide. z9

Also try... Amaryllis belladonna, Dierama pulcherrima, Limonium latifolium, Polygonum bistorta, Salvia superba

Annuals and Bedding Plants

Wallflowers (Cheiranthus) Excellent spring bedders flowering early and long in coastal areas and self-sowing happily. Sow late and transplant when not too large or the wind will rock them so much that the roots will suffer badly in winter.

The 'Bedder' series is at the shorter end of the height range at about 9–12in (23–30cm) and comes in a mixture of shades as well as separate colours such as primrose, gold, orange and red; growing about 18in (45cm) are varieties such as 'Blood Red', 'White Dame' in ivory white, 'Cloth of Gold' and 'Fire King' in orange scarlet. All produce their best scent after a little rain and in dry spells you can easily produce a short shower with the hose pipe.

Gazania Many years ago gazanias were raised from cuttings every year and a few plants kept over the winter in a frost-free greenhouse or frame as the plants are not quite hardy. In coastal areas they may well survive outside so that overwintering plants is unnecessary, while seed-raised strains are now available. The flowers are like huge single daisies in lovely fiery shades of mahogany, rust, orange, gold and yellow — sometimes with striped petals — on stout stems 6–15in (15–38cm) high.

Many of the old varieties such as 'Uniflora' have almost white felted foliage but unfortunately this is not a trait displayed by the seed-raised varieties. The names of the older sorts are rather confused so just pick those you like the sound of.

Amongst the seed-raised types two stand out. 'Mini-star', a short variety available in orange and tangerine plus a mixture of similar shades and 'Sundance' with a wonderfully coloured range of big flowers on larger plants. Many of the flowers are striped. Gazanias only open their flowers in the sunshine or on warm days so should be sited accordingly and also given a well-drained soil.

Petunia Half-hardy annuals often seen in municipal displays at seaside resorts. They won't take the full blast of the salt-laden wind but away from the front line they are very happy. The multiflora types such as 'Resisto Mixed' make an excellent choice and the 'Picotee' series in scarlet, blue, deep pink and purple each with a white rim is especially eye catching.

Also try... Dahlia (bedding types), *Glaucium flavum, Lavatera* species

6

SHADY GARDENS
DAMP SHADE — DRY SHADE

THE PROBLEM

In Britain where the climate is unpredictable and it's easy to believe there's never any sunshine, we worry if our gardens are shady. In the southern United States and other sunnier climes, shade is valued not only for the protection it gives to the overheated gardener taking a break but also for the protection it gives to plants. And for some plants it's vital in the same way that for others it spells death.

Obviously, the point about shade is that the light levels are low and this is exactly what many plants need. But there are different types of shade — shade can be cast by fences and walls or by the overhanging branches of deciduous and evergreen trees.

Shade from fences and buildings is different in character from that cast by trees. Fences and walls facing east and west are only in shadow for part of the day and, especially in summer, will receive good sunlight for many hours each day. A very large range of garden plants will grow in borders shaded in this way. But walls and fences facing north are different.

In winter, north facing borders will get virtually no sun at all. Even a light frost will persist all day in such a situation whereas a few yards away the soil will thaw very early in the morning. In summer when the sun is higher in the sky such borders often get a little direct sunlight early and late in the day when it shines along the length of the border from the side. Although the border is certainly in shade the amount of light reaching the plants is far greater than it would be if the area were overhung and such sites are often the best for shade loving plants. They are without the intense light of the sun yet are not dark and are without the competition from tree roots that accompanies shade from trees.

Shade from trees is very variable, depending on whether the tree sheds its leaves in winter and also on the type of shade cast by its leafy

Thoughtful removal of the lower branches can allow more light in under a large tree without destroying its attractive shape.

branches in summer. The way the tree is trained and pruned also makes a difference — just by removing the lower branches the amount of light filtering through can be greatly increased.

Evergreen trees provide the most difficult shade for plants to tolerate. Take a look at conifer plantations and at mature evergreens growing naturally and you find very little growing underneath. Trees like the evergreen oak (*Quercus ilex*) and the evergreen hollies (*Ilex*) cast very dense shade and only by sacrificing the shape and removing many of the lower branches can you let in enough light for plants to grow.

The shade cast by deciduous trees can vary enormously. The following trees cast very dense shade:

    Norway maple (*Acer platanoides*)
    horse chestnut (*Aesculus hippocastanum*)
    beech (*Fagus sylvatica*)
    flowering crab (*Malus*)
    red oak (*Quercus rubra*)
    Japanese cherries (*Prunus*)

These trees cast very light shade:
    paper bark maple (*Acer griseum*)
    birches (*Betula*)
    Pacific dogwood (*Cornus nutallii*)
    honey locust (*Gleditsia triacanthos*)
    mountain ash (*Sorbus aucuparia*)

You must also take into account the time when the trees actually come into leaf; a tree that starts to grow early in the year and develops a quick covering of foliage is going to cast shade for longer than a tree which comes into leaf later. Trees that shoot early include:

Norway maple
silver birch (*Betula pendula*)
hawthorn (*Crataegus monogyna*)
beech
flowering crab

Late leafers include:

paper bark maple
Indian bean tree (*Catalpa bignonoides*)
Pacific dogwood
Kentucky coffee tree (*Gymnocladus dioicus*)
Himalayan whitebeam (*Sorbus cuspidata*).

From this you can see that there's little similarity between similar trees and closely related species can have quite different leafing habits. Norway maple casts especially strong shade while the paper bark maple is a very light shader.

Generally speaking those trees which cast a very heavy shade are less favourable for those plants struggling to grow underneath than those which cast a lighter shade. And this means that trees with broad spreading crowns are less satisfactory than those with a more upright habit.

Most of the plants which thrive in shady borders do so because they are adapted to such situations in their wild homes. They tend to start to grow early in the year before the leaf canopy thickens and, like primroses (*Primula vulgaris*), flower very early, too, while there is still plenty of light. Some, like the winter aconite (*Eranthis hyemalis*), die back altogether by mid summer when the shade is at its most dense. Their reproductive cycle is also adapted to the setting. If conditions are moist the seeds may germinate as soon as they are shed but otherwise they wait until late winter or early spring, when they can have a relatively long growing season before the leaf canopy shuts out too much light.

Moist conditions usually accompany shade. Because a bed or border gets very little sun, water is lost both from foliage and from the soil surface more slowly so the soil is usually more moist. This tendency can be increased if leaves from shade trees are left on the beds, as they retain moisture. The problem arises with trees that steal a great deal of water and plant nutrients out of the soil, especially trees like sycamore (*Acer pseudoplatanus*), beech and birch with roots which run near the surface. Plants underneath can suffer very badly from both drought and starvation.

But here again the nature of the canopy is as important as the nature of the root system. Trees with a sparse branch structure cast less shade in the summer and also allow more light and water to filter through to the soil beneath. Trees with heavy canopies have so many leaves that water from light showers may never reach the ground. The droplets rest on the foliage then evaporate to the air. In winter, too, the relatively small number of branches not only lets through more light but more water. Dense trees often collect a substantial amount of water on the branches which runs back down the trunk and soaks into the soil at the bottom rather than soaking the ground further away.

DAMP SHADE: ALLEVIATING THE PROBLEM

If your shade is cast by a north facing wall or fence then you should be very grateful. See Chapter 7, on north and east facing walls, for plants to grow on the wall itself and select from the plants in this section. Plants in Chapter 12, on waterlogged soils, will also be useful if the soil conditions are heavy. To be honest, shade cast by walls is not a problem and if you steer clear of those suggested under south walls (Chapter 8), hot and dry conditions (Chapter 4) and most under stony soils (Chapter 11) you should have little trouble.

Deep shade cast by trees can be dealt with to some extent but care and thought are needed. It's best to think about this when you're planting trees. Just avoid those which cast a dense shade if you want to grow plants under them. Of course, you can treat a beech tree as the ultimate ground cover plant, for weeds won't grow under it, any more than garden plants will, but ensure that you think carefully if you plan to do this and put it in the right place.

Otherwise, avoid evergreen trees and those which cast a dense shade or leaf out especially early in the year. The smaller maples make especially good shade trees for smaller gardens.

If you're confronted by existing trees which are casting too much shade then some judicious pruning can help. And the operative word here is *judicious*. On no account allow yourself or some passing cowboy to hack away aimlessly with the vague hope of improving the situation. You can tackle small trees yourself but leave anything beyond the reach of a pair of domestic steps to the experts. You look at your trees every day of the year and if they're pruned badly they will be constantly offensive.

Thinning the crown is one way to let a little extra light through. This is no more than the careful removal of substantial branches at a point on or near the main trunk of the tree. The idea is to retain the overall shape of the tree and its natural form while simply thinning out the number of branches. It's best to examine the tree carefully in winter when the branch structure can be most clearly seen and mark branches that seem to need removal with white emulsion paint. It's then easier

A certain amount of judicious branch thinning can allow more rain and light through a tree to the plants growing below.

to imagine what the tree will look like without the marked branches. Never remove too many branches otherwise gales will get into the tree and may damage the remaining branches.

The branches should be removed in late winter except in the case of trees in the cherry family (*Prunus*) which should be cut in late spring. Ensure that you don't leave a stump and paint wounds with a wound sealant to prevent rotting.

Branches from low down on the tree can also be removed to let in more light. Some trees can be ruined by this treatment, like cedars and other conifers which rely on their full complement of branches to create their elegant appearance, but for oaks, limes, large maples and the like it can work well. As few branches as will solve the problem should be removed. Again, pruning should be done carefully — don't reduce the tree to little more than a tuft on a stick. Removing the lower branches also reduces the physical damage they can do to smaller plants as they sweep back and forth in summer breezes.

Amongst the shrubs recommended for shade are a number of evergreens. These are adapted to low light levels as their evergreen foliage enables them to make the most of winter and early spring light before the leaf canopy closes over. But planting too many will cast secondary shade which will reduce the amount of light for other plants, so don't overdo it.

DAMP SHADE: SOLVING THE PROBLEM WITH PLANTS

Trees

Planting more trees in an already shady spot is hardly guaranteed to improve the situation but in the shade of tall buildings, for example, it may be worthwhile.

If trees are appropriate the acid loving *Cercidiphyllum japonicum* (z5) with its astonishing autumn colour and modest proportions is a good choice. The bird cherry, *Prunus padus* (z4), is suitable with its drooping strings of almond-scented white flowers, followed by black berries. Hollies, too, especially varieties of *Ilex aquifolium* (z7) and *I.* × *altaclerensis* (z7) will thrive but most certainly add to the shade problem.

Hedges

Red chokeberry (Aronia arbutifolia) Rarely seen as a hedge in the UK, this relative of the pears and mountain ash nevertheless makes an attractive informal hedge for most soils except those which are shallow and limy. There are white flowers in spring, brilliant red fruits later and stunning autumn colours. The variety 'Erecta' is not only upright in habit but also especially dense in growth so is particularly suitable as a hedge. z5

Yew (Taxus baccata) Perhaps the best of all plants for garden hedges. The dense growth keeps out wind and intruders, the dark foliage is an ideal backdrop for flowers and its ability to grow not only in shade but in most soils that are not too soggy makes it a most adaptable plant. Add to that its suitability for topiary, as seen at Great Dixter in Sussex, and you have a very valuable plant.

This is another tree with male and female flowers on different plants but if it's going to be cut regularly you will get no berries anyway. Every part of the tree is poisonous except the red fleshy part of the fruit around the seed.

One thing to remember when planting a yew hedge, or any other garden hedge for that matter, is not to plant seedlings as they may vary slightly in vigour or colour. Use plants of a named variety or at least plants which have been raised from cuttings of the same plant. z6

Also try. . . Eleagnus ebbingei, Ilex, Rhododendron varieties

Shrubs

Maples (Acer palmatum) The maples include sycamores and sugar maples but many gardeners feel that these delightful, slow growing shrubs are the best choice.

They grow but slowly making broad, spreading, rounded hummocks of foliage which comes in various forms. At its simplest, it's five-fingered and green. But it can be far more finely cut, as in the variety 'Dissectum', and can be any shade from green to deep purple, as in 'Atropurpureum'. Put the two features together and you get — surprise, surprise — 'Dissectum Atropurpureum', one of the most delightful of small shrubs. z5

Camellia Exotic shrubs for shady spots though in dense shade flowering tends to wane. They will not, though, flower well in dry shade or in any dry spot. When the buds are forming in late summer moisture is essential and a dry period at that time will interrupt bud growth and in the spring the buds will drop off, leading you to blame it on the frost. Contrary to popular opinion of earlier this century camellias, and in particular *C. japonica*, are perfectly hardy — it just shows that public opinion can be very wrong.

There are many hundreds, thousands even, of varieties to choose from and most of those that are widely available will give a good account of themselves. My favourite? Well, I like the one everyone else likes, 'Donation', with rose pink, semi-double flowers. z7

Cephalotaxus harringtonia drupacea A close relative of the yew, from Japan, it differs noticeably in two ways. The leaves are longer and

Hosta 'Francis Williams' is one of the best and most attractive of newer varieties for foliage and flowering display in shady sites.

stand up from the branches in two ranks creating a V shape and the fruits, which appear in pairs, are about 1in (2.5cm) across and olive green in colour. This is a dense shrub with slightly drooping side branches and while not of outstanding beauty is nevertheless very attractive and unusual. A medium-sized shrub but again only the females carry the berries. z5

Spurge laurel (Daphne laureola) A small, evergreen British native shrub from woods mainly on alkaline soils. The flowers are yellow green in colour and nicely scented but are not showy. Many natural woodlanders combine evergreen foliage to make the most of sunlight early in the season, with early flowering and scent to attract pollinators — in this case flies and bumble bees. Many make valuable though not necessarily showy garden plants. z7

Fatsia japonica An excellent and wildly exotic shrub with big glossy fingered leaves giving a subtropical air to a shady corner. This effect is enhanced, in most people's eyes, by open heads of creamy white flowers in autumn when most other plants are giving up. An upright shrub, though not a large one, when mature giving a generally rounded outline. There is a form with white tips to the lobes of the foliage, 'Variegata'.

This plant has been crossed with ivy to give a valuable if rather floppy shade bearing plant called × *Fatshedera lizei*. This is the plant grown indoors as 'castor oil plant' although castor oil comes from the fruits of quite a different plant, *Ricinus communis*, with similar foliage. There is a variegated version with creamy yellow margins and both are worth evicting from the house to a more suitable residence outside. z7

Fothergilla major This relation of the more popular witch hazels is unjustly neglected. Flowering in spring as the leaves appear, the white clusters have a lovely fragrance. Later, in the autumn, is the other main burst of their beauty when the foliage turns yellow orange or scarlet before dropping. The only difficulty is that like rhododendrons these are acid loving or at least lime hating plants so will not thrive on alkaline soils. z5

Christmas box (Sarcococca) Now here's a plant to gladden the heart as you put your key in the lock on cold winter evenings. For the scent of this apparently unremarkable evergreen is really stunning. Every home should have one. There are a number of different types to be had and all have glossy pointed evergreen leaves, hardly reminiscent of the box at all. None has flowers which you would call exactly showy — they're small and peep out from the leaf joints in white or pink, but they appear in winter and the scent is wonderful.

S. *confusa* is my favourite and is one of the larger types, reaching about 4ft (1.2m) eventually, but taking a very long time to get there; the flowers are white. Only about half the height is S. *humilis* which is probably the best in shade and has pink flowers plus a useful suckering habit. Both have berries, both black. There are others which you may find. Don't buy them all, but buy one. z8

Sasa veitchii A rather invasive dwarf bamboo finds itself under this name — probably the only bamboo mentioned in this book but I haven't grown many. It has exceptionally broad leaves for a bamboo and colonises well with the extra advantage of the leaf edges turning greyish beige for the winter. z6

Schizophragma hydrangeoides A climbing member of the hydrangea family with the same requirements and similar flat, lacecap flower heads in creamy white. This can be a slow starter in life, and may need cosseting and talking to in its early years but then it will take off and can reach 40ft (12m) — it will happily grow up the trunk of the tree casting the shade. There is also a pink flowered form, 'Roseum'. z5

Viburnum davidii Well, another one of those 'berries only on females' plants — but what berries! Actually, it's a bit more complicated than that as some plants are almost entirely males and others almost entirely females. The crux of it is that you need a number of plants together to have a chance of the exquisite turquoise fruits held up above the glossy evergreen foliage in winter.

The plants are spreading and broad, not more than 2–3ft (60–90cm) high with unremarkable white flowers in late spring. If only the berries were produced a little more freely everyone would want one (sorry, four), but if you have the space give them a try. z7

Also try... Eleagnus pungens *'Maculata',* Euonymus fortunei *varieties,* Hypericum calycinum, Osmanthus × burk-woodii, Rhododendron *varieties*

Perennials

Lily of the valley (Convallaria majalis) The lily of the valley is a temperamental beast; sometimes it will settle down where you put it, increase steadily, flower well and you and the plant will be contented partners. Then again it may just languish neither increasing nor fading away entirely but pleasing no one; it may just die, of course. Its most curious behaviour is when it decides that the carefully chosen spot where you have placed it is not to its liking but another spot a little further down the border suits it rather better, and it packs its bags and migrates to what seems to the gardener to be an exactly similar spot where it thrives mightily.

So, quite what you have to do to please it is not entirely clear but I suggest moist shade but not too dark a spot. As well as the familiar species there are a number of varieties, the most easily obtainable of which are 'Fortin's Giant' with larger bells which appear a little later and 'Variegata' which usually sells at a ferocious price but which is worth it for the lovely narrow gold stripe along the leaf edges. z3

Bluebell (Endymion non-scriptus) The bluebell of the English woods is a wonderful plant creating a blue haze in spring when planted in large quantities. The easiest way to do just that is to plant some bulbs in the garden and collect the seed to scatter under your trees. As long as it's not too dry there should eventually be plenty of flowers though it must be said that a reasonably fertile soil is a great help to its success. What you must not do is pull the flowers out of the bulb — cut them off, but only from garden plants — or trample all over the foliage for this they just can't take. z6

Ferns I suppose I should really have put all the ferns in separately but as so many thrive in these conditions (most of which make good companions for the next items on the list) your choice of variety depends much on personal idiosyncrasy, so you find them all here.

First, my special favourites (it's my book after all) then a few others which I specially recommend. The shuttlecock fern, *Matteuccia struthiopteris* (z2), is a steady creeper which produces a short stem from which the fronds emerge. At first a clump looks just like a sunny forest of green shuttlecocks but as mid summer swings in they merge into a waving mass of upright fronds. Wonderful. The only thing that the shuttlecock fern must have is reasonable moisture.

The lady fern, *Athyrium filix-femina* (z4), is another favourite for the lacy delicacy of its fronds and *Dennstaedtia punctilobula* (z3) is like a miniature bracken running through the soil with the softest fresh fronds. Very pretty and not troublesome in spite of its habits.

Others to try are *Dryopteris pseudomas* (z5) and the many other species of male fern, *Polystichum setiferum* (z4) and the hart's tongue fern, *Asplenium scolopendrium* (z5).

Hostas In the American hosta world, things are really getting out of hand with huge numbers of varieties to be found and their names getting very confused indeed. In the UK things aren't quite as bad but the situation is still confusing. In spite of all that hostas are amongst the best of plants for shade, making dense weed-suppressing growth with foliage that varies from low, narrow and green, to broad, blue and tall.

Again, it's a matter of picking out a few favourites for guidance and leaving it to you. 'Thomas Hogg' (z4) is a well established variety which is not expensive and its leaves are widely margined with creamy white. It reaches about 2ft (60cm) and its lilac flowers are attractive, too, and appear early. Much smaller is *H. lancifolia* (z4) which has green leaves but to describe them as plain would be an insult. They are narrow and pointed, very glossy and they lie side by side, overlapping slightly like fish scales, in a very appealing way. There are lilac flowers, too, in autumn.

The third of the recommended trio is *H. sieboldiana* 'Elegans' (z3). This is big, bold and blue sometimes reaching 3ft (90cm) high with greyish blue rippled leaves up to 12in (30cm) across. The white flowers, which just peep through the foliage in stubby spikes, have a greyish tint, too. A dramatic and impressive plant that goes down well with most gardeners. There is also a splendid version with a bold gold edge to the leaf called 'Frances Williams' z4.

Solomon's seal (Polygonatum) There's nothing quite like the arching branches of solomon's seal, bringing quite a different form to the shady garden. The roots creep about just under the surface, sometimes a little too vigorously for comfort, and the stems rise up straight at first and then curve over to the horizontal so that the leaves on either side are horizontal too, and the long bells hang down conveniently where they can be seen.

There are a number of varieties around, the one usually found under *P. multiflorum* often being a hybrid but no worse for the confusion. It reaches 3ft (90cm) and like the others flowers in late spring, with up to five or six bells in a cluster. There is a variegated form greatly marred by the strongly undulating leaves. *P. odoratum* has fewer flowers, though they have a noticeable scent, but the variegated form is altogether superior with clear white margins. z4

Ramonda Rosette-forming plants related to African violets and very similar in appearance. A flat rosette of crinkly green foliage hugs the soil and in spring throws up open heads of flat, rounded flowers, usually in purplish blue, although there are also pink and white varieties occasionally seen. *R. myconi* is the one usually grown. It thrives in the cracks between bricks or peat blocks in low north facing walls and needs a soil that is rich in organic matter though well-drained. Like African violets ramonda can be increased by leaf cuttings. z7

Comfrey (Symphytum) Comfreys come in some variety, from fairly low ground coverers to tall and rampageous pests. *S. grandiflorum* is good low ground cover reaching 6–8in (15–23cm) with flowers in creamy white and it spreads well; there's a slightly taller blue variety, 'Hidcote', too. A variegated form with bluish flowers, 'Variegatum', is also occasionally seen.

The intensely impressive *S. × uplandicum* 'Variegatum' is altogether a different plant. It makes big early rosettes of foliage in greyish green with a broad band of pure cream around the edge. It's one of the best of all variegated plants but there is a tendency for it to revert to dark green. This must be dealt with promptly otherwise the whole plant, not to mention the rest of the garden, will quickly be swamped. The flowers on both the refined plant and the ruffian are pale blue. z3

Toad lily (Tricyrtis) These curious but very attractive plants would never be described as showy but the intricate markings on the flowers are very appealing. They reach 2–3ft (60–90cm) in slowly expanding clumps and in the autumn the stiff stems are topped with heads of unusually shaped flowers. *T. hirta* has flowers which are almost white with a dense purple spotting and *T. macropoda* is more creamy, also with purple spots. No description can do them justice. In colder areas a little sun is helpful. z5

Uvularia A beautiful early-flowering woodlander, *U. grandiflora* has fresh, slightly greyish foliage and pendulous yellow flowers. It spreads steadily and as the foliage expands later in the season makes a reasonable weed free cover. There is a variety, 'Pallida', with slightly larger, paler flowers. z3

Also try. . . Erythronium revolutum, Gentiana asclepiadea, Haberlea rhodopensis, Lilium martagon, Primula (candelabra types), Saxifraga fortunei, Smilacina racemosa

Annuals and Bedding Plants

Begonia The fibrous rooted begonias are amongst the few bedding plants which will produce a reasonable show in dense shade. It pays to choose the shorter varieties like 'Lucia' as the shade has a tendency to draw the plants up making a more diffuse display. Most mixtures have some plants with bronze foliage, which in a darkish place does not always intensify the display, but mixtures with only green leaves are hard to find. 'Verdo' is one you may come across. Some companies sell 'Organdie Mixed' with only green leaves, others sell it with green and bronze. 'Thousand Wonders White' has large white flowers and pale green foliage and will brighten any shady corner.

Busy lizzies (Impatiens) The supreme shade lovers, a wonderful range of colours is available on plants which stay fairly neat. Again, start out with dwarfer types like 'Super Elfin' or 'Mini' unless you especially want large plants in which case 'Blitz' is the one to go for. And again, if you choose separate colours, choose carefully as some of the reds are rather dusky and have dark, dull foliage, too. The pinks, lilacs and white are the most lively choices for shade plus those with flowers enlivened with a white star.

Also try. . . Mimulus varieties, Nemophila insignis

DRY SHADE: ALLEVIATING THE PROBLEM

Even if the level of shade is acceptable, or you've made it acceptable by some of the methods outlined earlier, if tree roots are near to the surface or the trees themselves are especially greedy, the soil can be so dry that only a limited range of plants will thrive. Improving the moisture level is therefore the priority.

Building raised beds under the trees has been tried successfully by some gardeners. These beds are most suitably made using logs, logroll or peat blocks rather than stone, brick or concrete. They can be made up to about 2ft (60cm) high, perhaps with a lower section at the front, but the soil that fills them should never be piled against the trunk of the tree as the tree may well be killed.

The bed should be filled with a moisture retentive compost such as 2 parts by volume of good garden soil, 1 part grit, 1 part peat and 1 part leaf mould. Even if you don't make a raised bed the soil can be improved by forking in peat or leaf mould or, if you've got a clay patch in the garden, by adding some heavy soil from there to retain moisture.

Watering is another option and the keen grower of the more choice shade plants may well want to install a permanent watering system which can be switched on from a distance and which automatically does the job. The most important thing about watering is that it should be thorough. If you only give small quantities of water the tree roots

Raised beds can easily be constructed using sawn poles. Fork over the base before filling with soil mixture.

Shrubs and trailing plants can then be set in place before final planting.

will creep towards the surface looking for it and the whole area will soon be full of roots. So leave the sprinkler on for at least an hour and a half.

Watering is a vital part of thorough care at planting time for all plants in this situation. Planting sites should be improved with organic matter and you can even remove a few selected tree roots if it's done carefully. Water after planting to help rapid establishment combined, if you like, with a liquid feed.

Whether you build a raised bed or simply improve the soil an annual mulch of peat or leaf mould will make a big difference. This will retain plenty of moisture and, in the case of leaf mould, rot down slowly steadily releasing nutrients to the plants. And all these trees which are creating such a problem will be providing plenty of leaves with which to make leaf mould.

DRY SHADE: SOLVING THE PROBLEM WITH PLANTS

The plants I have suggested for dry shade are those that will survive relatively unimproved conditions. If you put a lot of effort into improving the situation then the shade is unlikely to be so dense or the soil so dry that you can't grow a far wider range of plants.

Trees

Few sane gardeners will plant trees in an area of dry shade as they will only make the situation worse. But there's always one or two, so if you're one of the few I can suggest the field maple, *Acer campestre* (z5), a tree which casts only a light shade and stands shade, too. Its autumn colour is perhaps its most attractive feature. The other choice should be the honey locust, *Gleditsia triacanthos* (z5), which although a large tree has an open habit and there is a good yellow-leaved version — 'Sunburst'.

Hedges

Berberis × stenophylla This is a hybrid between the splendid *B. darwinii* and the dwarf *B. empetrifolia*. It makes a rather spiny but very attractive flowering hedge with arching sprays of yellow flowers in spring. By clipping it to shape *immediately* flowering is over there is a good chance of a second flush of flowers later in the year. The foliage is narrow and dark and it makes a singularly impenetrable barrier, the deterrent effect of which is heightened by the accumulation of dead spines in the hedge bottom. Not a hedge to plant if there are children about but good for keeping next door's dog at bay. If you're feeling positively sadistic, you poor soul, then *B. gagnepanii*, with spines up to 2in (5cm) long, may be the answer but this should not be planted thoughtlessly. z6

A woodland planting with azaleas, trillums, primulas, rodgersias and hostas growing in light shade and moist soil.

Snowberry (Symphoricarpus) A rather twiggy, slightly grey-leaved shrub reaching about 4–5ft (1.2–1.5m) making an attractive informal hedge. The flowers are more or less insignificant but the fruits are impressive and what's more the birds leave them alone. There are a number of varieties but the white-fruited 'White Hedge' is specially recommended for hedging and should be planted 18in (45cm) apart. z4

Also try. . . *Buxus sempervirens*

Shrubs

Berberis wilsoniae This delightful small shrub is dense and spiny and good for dryish soils in sun or shade. It's in the autumn that it's at its best. The bluish green, rounded foliage is attractive from its first opening in spring and then starts to colour, taking on lovely pinkish shades and at the same time the fruits colour up, often in matching shades. z6

Cotoneaster 'Cornubia' A large spreading shrub or small tree depending how it's trained, the arching growth is attractive with long evergreen foliage and white flowers in spring. Later in the year the huge berries appear, in fat bunches, making a dramatic sight in autumn. This is one of the most impressive of all fruiting shrubs and the branches cover the ground well, suppressing weeds and providing a good background to other plants. z6

Danae racemosa A small evergreen shrub in the lily family (if you find the idea surprising there's another coming up) that seems to thrive in this particular problem place. The leaves are rather shiny and carried in arching sprays. With luck you'll get orange berries in the autumn. This is an especially good shrub for cutting for flower arrangements as the foliage is conveniently long lasting. Not an outstanding garden plant by any means — some dismiss it unjustly as boring — but unusual and useful. z7

Euonymus This is a very large group but just two species interest us in this section, *E. fortunei* and to a lesser extent *E. japonicus*. *E. fortunei* comes in many guises but the most familiar are the more or less prostrate variegated varieties. 'Emerald 'n' Gold' has become especially widely grown in recent years, its leaves are dark with gold variegations and a touch of bronze in winter. 'Silver Queen' is altogether paler with silvery variegation and pinkish winter tints – a real favourite. 'Silver Queen' will also climb a tree trunk, albeit slowly, if it happens to meet one on its otherwise horizontal travels. There are more; look at them and choose one you like — even the plain green ones are attractive.

On a larger scale are the varieties of *E. japonicus* of which there are rather fewer. They are all larger-leaved and larger in growth than *E. fortunei* and two variegated ones stand out. 'Aureus' has almost entirely yellow leaves with only a narrow green line round the edge of the leaf while 'Aureopictus' has a much broader green margin. z8

Garrya elliptica One of the most reliable of winter-flowering shrubs, though its flowers are in the form of greyish green catkins. They are especially showy on male plants, but the fruits on the females, which are round and come in short strings, are also attractive. The best male variety is called 'James Roof' with its especially long catkins. Reaching 10–12ft (3–3.6m) its evergreen foliage is greyish in colour and slightly toothed and it's a cheering sight in winter and early spring. z7

Ivy (Hedera) Useful for both ground cover and climbing, the ivies are ideal shade plants. To be at their best as ground cover in dry shade they should be planted so that their roots are in soil that is as moist as it can be and then trained so that the shoots creep into the drier area. The best for this treatment is *H. helix* 'Hibernica' with especially large dark leaves.

With good preparation, other forms, especially the variegated ones like 'Glacier' with white markings and 'Gold Heart' with a yellow splash, can be encouraged and will not only cover the ground prettily but also clothe the trunk of the tree casting the shade. z5

Lonicera pileata An increasingly widely grown shrub which is almost evergreen but usually not quite. The narrow, dark green leaves are carried on horizontal shoots giving an unusual appearance and the pale young shoots overlaying the older darker leaves are very attractive. Berries are occasionally produced but it must be said that you have to be lucky to see them. If you do, they will be a semi-transparent lilac shade but don't get too worked up about them in advance, because they might never appear. z7

Oregon grape (Mahonia aquifolium) No prizes for guessing where this plant hails from although in fact it grows all along that west coast of America. It's an agreeably adaptable, rather floppy, evergreen plant, thriving in a wide range of situations including dry shade. The combination of the slightly purplish winter foliage and the clusters of yellow flowers which start to appear in late winter has always been appreciated. Even in less hospitable spots it tends to spread via the black berries which give it its name. z5

Rubus tricolor A prostrate growing ornamental bramble whose chief glories are its stems and its glossy foliage which are covered in red bristles. One reference book describes this plant as 'a benign galloper' and 'possibly the fastest of all ground coverers in shade'. Fortunately,

Variegated comfrey makes a bright rosette of leaves in spring and follows it up with this attractive combination of flowers and foliage.

dry shade slows it up a little but it really is aggressive, rooting as it goes. It carries single white flowers in summer and may just treat you to a few red fruits later in the year. A good carpet in the most difficult conditions, even doing well under beech trees. z7

Butcher's broom (Ruscus) This is the other bushy member of the lily family and an altogether more familiar one. The leaves are a little fresher in colour than those of *Danae racemosa* but it has the additional complication of having male and female flowers on different plants (though there is a very rare hermaphrodite form). So, if you are particular about seeing the red berries you must make sure you have both sexes. There are two species grown, one a great deal more often than the other.

Ruscus aculeatus hails from southern Europe including southern England and is upright in growth spreading slowly by suckers. *R. hypoglossum* from a little further south is more spreading in habit and has larger foliage. Both are worth growing as they thrive in conditions which other plants would shrivel at the sight of. z7

Skimmia Personally there's only one skimmia I have any time for, S. *japonica* 'Rubella'. This is a hard judgement I know and for the sake of less dogmatic gardeners I shall mention some of the others, but let's start with the best.

This is a slow growing, dark foliaged plant, rather upright in habit with leaves like a holly only without the spines. The flower buds appear in the autumn like tiny bunches of red grapes held at the tips of the shoots and they sit there all winter looking pending. Then in early spring they open to reveal pretty white flowers. Skimmias too have male and female flowers on different plants and S. *japonica* 'Rubella' is sadly a male — but you can't have everything.

If it's berries you fancy then S. *japonica* 'Foremannii' is the one you should try as it produces them with especial freedom and in a particularly large and luscious red. My argument with this and most of the others is that the foliage so often looks pale and anaemic and this detracts from the fruits which are their chief appeal. 'Nymans' and 'Rogersii' are also good fruiters. z7

Also try. . . Aucuba japonica, Ilex, Sambucus

Perennials

Bear's breeches (Acanthus) Large imposing plants with a substantial architectural quality that would enhance a lot of gardens. It must be said that they are at their best out in the sun and will not flower so prolifically in the shade but their foliage is nevertheless so magnificent that they are worth growing just the same.

The most widely seen is A. *mollis* 'Latifolius' (z7) with huge shining leaves arching dramatically but few flowers. If you prefer something a little more spiny go for A. *spinosus* (z8) or if you've got a real thing about spines then A. *spinosissimus* (z8) is the plant for you.

Surprisingly, these plants can be a little on the tender side so plant in spring and mulch well with leaf mould each autumn as a protection.

Lady's mantle (Alchemilla mollis) A wonderful plant in what was once a very unfashionable colour and now only suffering from being planted too often and allowed to seed too much.

In spring the young leaves unfurl and the hairs retain glistening droplets of water in the same way as those of lupins. As they open more they can be seen to be a lovely downy green and then the very pale olive heads of lacy flowers on lax stems follow. I must say that it's wise counsel to cut off the flower heads before they set seed otherwise the whole garden will be full of seedlings. You can cut the foliage back hard at the same time and it will re-grow as fresh as spring. z3

Euphorbia robbiae Now correctly called E. *amygdaloides* var. *robbiae*, but I doubt if it will ever be changed in catalogues so I won't change it here. Dark green leaves and heads of olive flowers early in the year plus the ability to sucker steadily make this a valuable plant, although it can get straggly, so cut it back hard after flowering and it will regenerate well. z7

Stinking gladdon (Iris foetidissima) A curious name for a straightforward plant which in Britain grows in open woods, usually on alkaline soils. It also grows in slightly less open woods and produces tufts of dark foliage about 18in (45cm) high which is said to smell of roast beef — though it's a matter of opinion. The flowers are small and prettily marked in purple with a little yellow and white. The fruits are more striking when the pods burst to reveal rows of bright orange seeds.

There is a version called 'Citrina' which is larger in every respect and has pale yellow and lilac flowers and there is also 'Variegata' which sacrifices the flowers and seed pods for cream stripes in the foliage. z6

Archangel (Lamiastrum galeobdolon) A close relative of the dead nettles, the main differences are the altogether taller and more vigorous growth and the yellow flowers. 'Variegatum', with irregular silvery markings on the leaves, is very attractive, though also very vigorous, while 'Silver Carpet' has white veins and is much slower in growth and less suited to dry shade. z4

Dead nettle (Lamium maculatum) These are amongst my favourite low growing spreaders making attractive carpets of white splashed foliage and, in spring, sheets of flowers in magenta, pink or white. The leaves are nettle-shaped, though rather smaller, but don't sting — hence the name. The original variety has dark leaves with a central white stripe and magenta flowers; 'Album' is the same with white flowers and 'Roseum' with pink flowers. 'Chequers' has a broader white splash and magenta flowers, 'Beacon Silver' has the same flowers and leaves almost entirely white, while 'White Nancy' is similar with white flowers and 'Silver Dollar' the same with dark pink flowers. On top of those there is 'Aureum' with yellow leaves, faintly striped with white and sparsely produced magenta flowers — this is relatively weak in growth; 'Beedham's White' is yellow with white flowers. There is also a version with pure yellow leaves.

All creep well, rooting as they go and do much of their growing early in the year. z3

Liriope Dense tufted plants with broad grass-like foliage making dense clumps. The purple flowers appear in late summer and last well into autumn and come in stiff upright spikes densely packed with flowers reminiscent of a grape hyacinth. L. muscari, sometimes known as L. platyphylla, is the variety normally found although L. spicata is occasionally seen. This is altogether shorter in growth and earlier to flower and tends to creep rather than form clumps. z6

Periwinkle (Vinca) There are two main kinds suitable for this situation, the greater and the lesser, *V. major* (z7) and *V. minor* (z5).

The greater periwinkle is a vigorous plant with pairs of large oval leaves along stems which either run along the surface of the ground for great distances or arch over and root at the tips. Large pale blue flowers appear at the centre of the clumps in early spring though in a rather unpredictable manner. 'Elegantissima' with creamy yellow variegations is a great brightener of dark, dry corners under trees.

The lesser is lesser in every way — smaller leaves and flowers and more restrained growth. In the ordinary variety the leaves are dark and the flowers light blue. There are many other varieties including the most attractive 'Variegata Aurea' with gold markings and 'Alba' with white flowers. The former especially makes a pretty winter carpet of foliage, soft and bright but not coarse.

Waldsteinia ternata This is a sort of rampageous strawberry which makes dense carpets of dark foliage doing a great job at snuffing out all but the most tenacious weeds. There are also yellow, strawberry-like flowers in spring but sadly no red juicy fruits. Visitors are often surprised to see what appears to be a dense mat of strawberry plants producing flowers like buttercups so it's worth growing just for that. z5

Also try... Carex pendula, Dryopteris filix-mas, Epimedium species, *Polystichum setiferum, Trachystemon orientale*

Annuals and Bedding Plants

Honesty (Lunaria annua) This is a difficult situation for annual plants and few will make a go of things in such conditions but honesty is one. It's generally a biennial which self-sows — albeit not aggressively in this dry site. The flowers are purple but there is also a white and a horrid version with white splashed foliage. After the flowers come the silvery flat seed pods, much used for dried arrangements indoors.

Smyrnium perfoliatum At first sight this looks like a spurge with its pale olive flower heads but in fact it's a delightful member of the carrot family. A biennial, it reaches about 2ft (60cm) in height and flowers in early summer, seeding itself about when happy, making large colonies.

7

NORTH AND EAST FACING WALLS AND FENCES

THE PROBLEM

Gardeners tend to divide themselves into two groups — those who see walls as a problem and those who see that they can be used to add greater interest and diversity to the garden. Both are right. Gardeners who don't make the most of their walls and fences are missing a big opportunity but there are problems which must be remembered, or maybe solved, if plants are to thrive.

The first problem is sun — on north walls it's the almost total lack of sun and on east walls it's the fact that what sun there is strikes first thing in the morning.

A north facing wall or fence gets almost no sun at all except in summer, when in the morning and evening the sun sometimes shines along its length. This is much less of a difficulty than an area shaded from above by a tree as, although a north facing border gets no sun, it is still light, whereas an overhung border can be very dark indeed. There are many plants which will be happy on a north facing wall or in a north facing border that will not grow under trees.

An east facing wall or fence has the same problem and the fact that it gets sun first thing in the morning is not necessarily an advantage. In winter the coldest nights tend to be very clear and by morning stems, foliage and buds are well frozen; this in itself is not always harmful as long as the thaw is slow. But when the sun strikes first thing in the morning frozen growth often thaws out so quickly that plant cells are ruptured and growth killed. Buds and blossoms are especially susceptible.

Of course, without much sun both north and east walls are cold; as I write, my long north facing border has been continuously white with frost for almost a week whereas on the opposite side of my narrow garden the frost is gone by midday and penetrates much less. Growth starts a little later in the spring and finishes a little earlier in the autumn — a clump of the same variety of daffodils planted 10yd (9m) apart facing north and south will differ in flowering time by a week or even two. Many plants will grow quite happily when facing north or east but especially on a north aspect the lack of sun may dramatically reduce their flowering; most roses are good examples.

Wind is another facet of the problem, especially when combined with cold. This has two effects. In winter, north and east winds are not only cold in themselves but increase the chill factor so that growth is more liable to damage. Wind also increases the evaporation from evergreens, though this is not a problem when plenty of moisture is available to replenish it. But when the soil is frozen, even if the roots do not suffer from the frost, they can't take up water so as the top growth loses moisture to the wind it can't be replenished.

Moisture can be a pain or a blessing in other ways. With little or no sun soil takes a long time to dry out. In summer this can be an advantage to plants which would suffer from drought in other parts of the garden. But in winter a wet soil is more harmful than a dry one and can be a significant cause of losses.

Finally, the soil at the foot of walls of all aspects can be drier or wetter than soil in the open at different times. When rain is driving against a wall it runs down and soaks the soil at the base; conversely, a wall or fence can prevent water soaking a border if the rain is driving the other way.

The self-clinging climbing hydrangea, Hydrangea petiolaris, *is slow growing in its early years but the flowers are worth waiting for.*

ALLEVIATING THE PROBLEM

Most of these difficulties cannot be solved — you can't argue with nature. But there are plenty of plants which will thrive in such conditions if you choose the right ones. The wind problem is probably the easiest to deal with and the planting of some suitable evergreens, probably conifers, at strategic points can be a great help. If in your garden the prevailing wind is such that the soil at the base of north and east walls tends to lie very wet then the addition of some grit can make enough difference to the range of plants which can be grown — and if it stays dry, organic matter will help.

SOLVING THE PROBLEM WITH PLANTS

Wall Shrubs

Azara microphylla A fresh foliaged evergreen, once thought to be tender but now proved the hardiest of the group. Not for east walls, but for north walls near a path the early spring flowers with their wonderful vanilla scent are a real delight. Eventually this can grow beyond shrub size and make a small tree but a little careful and thoughtful pruning after flowering can ensure that it doesn't outgrow its space — if space is a problem. There is a variegated form, 'Variegata', with creamy markings but it's noticeably less vigorous. z8

Japonica (Chaenomales) Good on north or east aspects, they can be trained fairly flat by removing shoots growing away from the wall after flowering and thinning and tying in other shoots evenly. They can also be allowed to bush out and form a rounded plant. Flowering in late winter and spring on the bare branches, 'Nivalis' is white, 'Knap Hill Scarlet' is orangey scarlet and very bright, 'Rowallane' is deep red and 'Moerloosei' is apple blossom pink.

Although often called quinces these varieties will only produce relatively small fruit, and not regularly. For fruiting, *Cydonia oblonga*, with very pale pink flowers, is the one to grow and it will do well on a north or east wall but is inclined to outgrow its space and needs pruning annually to fruit well. z5

Itea ilicifolia Not for east facing walls but thriving if facing north, this elegant evergreen has large, glossy, holly-like leaves and long tassels of greenish white flowers in summer. The young growth has a bronzish tinge. Sometimes recommended for south walls, this reveals an unnecessarily cautious attitude in most areas. The early morning sun burns the frozen growth. z7

Jasmine (Jasminum) The ever popular winter jasmine, *J. nudiflorum* (z5), may not seem to be the most elegant of plants but its sunny flowers are so welcome in the depths of winter that no garden can afford to be without it. And indeed it only looks scrappy when it's not trained effectively.

The way to keep it looking good is to train shoots evenly up the wall and tie them in, from these the flowering shoots will grow, billowing downwards appealingly. After flowering these shoots must be cut back hard to an inch or two and from the remaining buds will grow the shoots to provide the following year's flowers. Cut for the house while still in bud. Good when facing north or east. *J. mesnyi* (z7), also known as *J. primulinum*, has been recommended for east walls — ignore this advice or waste your money.

Firethorn (Pyracantha) An excellent wall shrub for a north or east facing site. Although the evergreen leaves are rather dark and dull, the heads of white flowers in spring and the berries which follow later give a double display, always important in a sunless spot. It should be trained to give a broad framework and then thinned back after flowering or after fruiting. Mature plants are favourite sites for nesting birds.

Three varieties are commonly planted; 'Lalandei' has relatively pale berries in orange, 'Orange Glow' also has orange fruits but is very vigorous and 'Watereri' has bright red berries. 'Watereri' makes an especially good wall plant. Superseding 'Lalandei' is 'Mojave' with slightly darker berries plus the added bonus of resistance to fireblight and scab. Other varieties are available with berries ranging from yellow to the darkest red. z6

Also try... Camellia varieties (north wall only), *Garrya elliptica, Jasminum humile, Osmanthus delavayi, Piptanthus laburnifolius*

Climbers

Dutchman's pipe (Aristolochia macrophylla) The big, rather rough, heart-shaped leaves are in themselves attractive but have the sad and serious fault of hiding the extraordinary flowers — which are shaped like an old fashioned curved pipe; they're olive green but brown at the mouth, appear in late spring and always come in pairs. This is a vigorous plant, which needs plenty of space to do it justice so it's a great shame to prune it too much. z6

Ercilla volubis Self clinging climbers are relatively few in number compared with twiners and this unusual climber from China is one which should be grown more often. The leaves are pale green and rather leathery and succulent and in spring short spikes of pinkish white flowers appear. This is a vigorous plant when established and better suited to a house wall than a low boundary wall. z8

Euonymus A number of the varieties of *E. fortunei* can be persuaded to climb and once they get going cling quite well by aerial roots, although they sometimes take a little persuading. On walls, a piece of Elastoplast or Band-Aid can be used to encourage progress in the right direction by fixing stems to the wall in appropriate places. 'Silver Queen' is the best choice with small green foliage, each leaf with a creamy margin. In spring the young shoots are creamy yellow. 'Variegatus', sometimes called 'Gracilis', has a pink tinge to the leaves and can also usually be persuaded to climb. Neither will reach more than 6ft (1.8m) and both will be slow getting there. z5

Ivies (Hedera) Favourite self clinging wall coverers, some can be so oppressive and dull in sunless places that they depress the whole household. Some of the large-leaved types, though colourful, are rather coarse. I prefer the small-leaved types with delicate colouring or interesting leaf shapes which do more than just cover the bricks. All are respectable self clingers, needing a little assistance in the early stages, and they only damage the oldest brickwork and soft mortar. Otherwise they're a positive benefit, shedding water away from the wall very well.

Most of those available are varieties of *Hedera helix* (z5). 'Glacier' is one of my favourites and has leaves in varying but attractive shades of greyish green with a fine white margin; the leaves are of a clear sharp shape, softened by the slightly variable margin. 'Gold Heart' has a big bold yellow splash on dark green leaves and 'Buttercup' is pure soft yellow, eventually aging to green with yellow veins.

The larger-leaved types, which are also significantly more vigorous, are based on *H. canariensis* (z7), which is sometimes rendered less than elegant by severe winters, though usually survives, and on *H. colchica* (z5). The popular 'Gloire de Marengo' is a variety of the former with large rolled leaves with silvery green variegations and yellow edges; the young leaves are the most striking. 'Dentata Variegata' is a very impressive form of *H. colchica* with greyish shading to the leaves and a deep creamy margin varying from a thin line to most of the leaf. 'Sulphur Heart', also known as 'Paddy's Pride' and 'Gold Leaf', is also variable, and may simply have yellow veins or a rather ragged and central area of yellow.

Hydrangea Gardeners familiar with the mophead hydrangea may be unaware of the climbing version, *Hydrangea petiolaris*, although the resemblance of the flowers to the lacecap types will give it away. It has the benefit of being a self clinging type but the disadvantage of making a very slow start to life and only getting down to some decent covering after gathering its strength. The white flowers are broad, lacecap in

The white-variegated ivy 'Glacier' brightens many a dull corner with its attractive foliage.

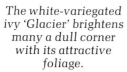

Many clematis, like this 'Lady Northcliffe', thrive on north walls where their flowers fade less than in sunnier situations.

form and the bark, on mature plants, peels off in attractive pale chestnut strands.

It flowers especially well on a north wall but may need guidance as to where to climb. z4

Sweet pea (Lathyrus) Both the perennial and annual types fit here. The everlasting pea, L. *latifolius* (z5), is a real toughie although it dies down every winter. The flowers are smaller than the annual sweet pea but come in loose spikes of up to 15 flowers. Purplish pink, pale pink and white forms are available and they can easily be raised from seed.

There is also L. *grandiflorus* (z6) with much larger purple flowers, though fewer of them and smaller heads and although the flowers last only a day or two they keep coming.

Annual sweet peas, L. *odoratus* (z3), need little discussion as they're so familiar except to say that you will probably find that the pale shades do especially well facing north or east as they will not be bleached. Sow in autumn in pots and plant in spring and sow in spring alongside the autumn-sown plants for the longest display.

Virginia creeper (Parthenocissus) The true Virginia creeper is P. *quinquefolia* (z3) although other species are sometimes given the same name. The true plant is a vigorous self clinging climber, frequently covering gable ends of houses or even every available area of brickwork. Its riotous crimson autumn colour is its big attraction although the ease with which it grows is also valuable. P. *tricuspidata* (z4), from Japan and China, is often seen as Virginia creeper and is also known as Boston ivy and Japanese creeper. It has lovely glossy leaves

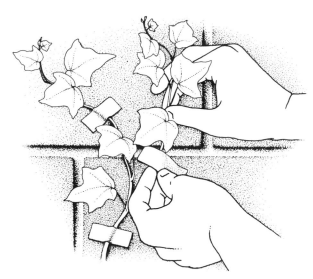

Self-clinging climbers often need encouragement in their early stages and sticky tape can help guide them in the right direction.

which vary in shape on the same plant whereas the Virginia creeper has dull leaves. The autumn colour is equally intense.

My favourite is *P. henryana* (z7) which has fingered leaves of a very unusual greenish bronze with the veins picked out in white. Very attractive though slow to get going in my garden, quicker elsewhere, so it must be me!

Pilostegia viburnoides Another of the small band of self clinging climbers which, with white flowers like those of a lacecap hydrangea, has the extra advantage of being evergreen and is especially happy on shady walls. The flowers appear in late summer and come in pyramidal clusters. A slow-growing plant but worth waiting for. z7

Rose (Rosa) There is a limited selection of roses which thrive on north walls and they are all climbers; most will grow well but flower poorly, but some will flower well. 'Danse du Feu' is a strong, vigorous plant with slightly orangey red flowers which unfortunately take on a purplish tinge as they age. 'Guinee' is darker but for these situations a paler one is more useful. 'Madame Alfred Carriere' has pale pink buds opening to white flowers all summer and is a wonderful plant; 'Madame Gregoire Staechlin' is pink with an astonishing scent but unfortunately it flowers for only a short period. (z5)

Schisandra grandiflora An unusual and uncommon twining climber usually only available in its variety 'Rubriflora'. But its rarity is not a true measure of its charm; it should be grown more often. The flowers are about 1in (2.5cm) across and hang from pendulous stalks. They appear in late spring and are deep red and slightly fragrant; the males and females appear on different plants so to get the bright red berries plants of both sexes should be planted together. z7

Canary creeper (Tropaeolum perigrinum) An easy annual with small fingered leaves and bright yellow, slightly feathery flowers. Best planted under stout shrubs through which it can scramble, it grips its host by twisting its leaf stem around the twigs. It can be sown where it is to flower and the base of a pyracantha is a good spot as it flowers as the berries of the pyracantha are reddening.

Also try. . . Akebia quinata, Celastrus orbiculatus, Clematis varieties, Cotoneaster horizontalis, Lonicera japonica 'Aureo- reticulata'

8

SOUTH FACING
WALLS AND FENCES

THE PROBLEM

In the case of south facing walls, the opportunities really do outweigh the problems — though problems there are and they should not be underestimated. But south facing walls provide the exciting opportunity to grow exotic and slightly tender plants for which conditions in the rest of the garden are just too cold and exposed.

A wall, or even a fence, facing south catches all the sun going so that frosts set in less readily on winter evenings, thaw more quickly in the morning and penetrate less deeply. Brick and stone walls in particular hold a substantial residue of heat which protects plants from harmful chills. There is also protection from cold winds from the east and north.

But this baking does produce difficulties. In summer the soil is often extremely dry as it loses water by increased evaporation from the soil surface as well as indirectly through increased transpiration through the leaves of the plants, and this moisture, too, must come from the soil. So plants chosen for this site should not only need the protection of a little warmth in winter but should also be able to withstand what can be rather harsh conditions in summer. The Chilean bellflower (Lapageria rosea) is a prime example of a plant which is tender but also needs a moist soil in summer so will not thrive in this site.

Any plants which are set too close to the wall are liable to remain dry for longer periods than those planted a little further into the border and then trained back to the wall; this can make the creation of an even, attractive fan shape more difficult.

The long days of sunshine have another effect. Plants with flowers in soft colours — sweet peas and clematis spring to mind — often bleach in such bright conditions so that pink and lilac shades become much less intense, indeed rather watery and thin.

Moisture and plant foods can cause problems, too. When the soil is baked in summer its organic matter is broken down so quickly that it does not provide the reservoir of water which would be so valuable. In these circumstances plants which would otherwise thrive wilt at the tips and lose their lower leaves — not a very appealing sight. Flowering may be curtailed and unless the right plants are chosen the effect can be rather ragged. When organic matter is burnt up plant foods are released into the soil so that when there is a wet spell, and in the UK the prevailing wet wind is from the south west so the wall will gather an especially large proportion of it, the nutrients are leached through quickly.

ALLEVIATING THE PROBLEM

As you can see the warmth of the wall brings problems as well as advantages. If the plants are sheltered from the worst of the sun in summer then they will not receive its benefit in winter. For some plants, watering in summer can be a great help but if you grow plants that need a good baking in the border at the foot of the wall, particularly species tulips and bulbous irises, these will not thrive in these artificially moist conditions.

The usual recommendation is not to water in the heat of the day but for many plants the leaf scorch that was feared causes little or no damage and in the days when this advice was at its most fervent, gardens were looked after by paid gardeners who could be persuaded or cajoled to come in early in the morning or stay late in the evening to water at the correct time. Now, although for people in work the evening is usually the most convenient time to water in summer, we tend to lead busier lives and the watering gets done when there is time.

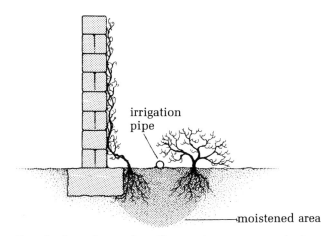

irrigation pipe

moistened area

The soil at the foot of a south wall sometimes gets very dry but a seep hose laid on the soil can provide valuable extra moisture.

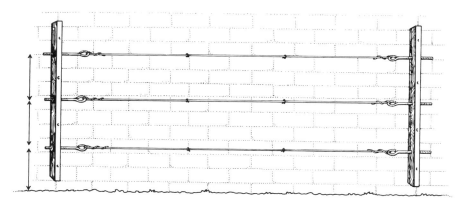

It pays to wire walls properly if climbers and wall shrubs are to be grown and battens with eye bolts provide an effective method.

Fortunately, the arrival of automatic timers to control the watering make it a lot more convenient.

Whenever possible it pays to plant 12–15in (30–38cm) out from the foot of the wall as against the wall the soil is often dust dry for long periods.

Organic matter is usually a big help in conserving water although if you grow a lot of grey foliage plants in the border and your soil is naturally heavy, the soil may lie too wet for them. In that case you may lose plants not from frost but from excessive moisture more often than you would like.

Lack of nutrients can easily be remedied but the fertiliser should be chosen carefully as plants which are susceptible to cold and winter rots will be made more vulnerable if they are fed with a fertiliser which contains too much nitrogen (N). A formulation such as En-Mag, John Innes Base or Chempak BTD, anything with a relatively low nitrogen content, is preferable.

The problem of how to give plants on a warm wall the warmth they need, provide protection from wind, and keep them reasonably moist has been dealt with cleverly at the garden at Mount Usher, in County Wicklow south of Dublin in the Irish Republic. Spaced along the wall are brick built, flying buttress-like additions at right angles to the wall itself. These provide cosy corners in which plants can nestle. Part of the area is also sheltered by shrubs set in irregular groups a little distance from the wall. This protects the plants from wind, makes a sheltered pocket free from frost and protects plants from the low early morning sun in winter but allows it to shine over the top to the wall plants in summer. In this area bananas are grown, quite something for a garden on the same latitude as Labrador.

SOLVING THE PROBLEM WITH PLANTS

Wall Shrubs

Abeliophyllum distichum A choice, though rather slow growing, winter-flowering shrub which needs a hot summer to ripen the shoots and promote generous flowering the following winter. It's not tender but needs the warmth of a south wall to ensure that the shoots get the thorough ripening they need to flower well and is usually at its best after a hot summer. It's a deciduous shrub with four-petalled white flowers tinged with palest pink which may be tipped by frost if the cold snap is especially sudden. It looks rather like a white forsythia. z4

Mimosa or wattle (Acacia) A very large group of shrubs and trees with about 800 species, mostly originating in Australia. The toughest are probably the silver wattle or mimosa, *A. dealbata*, and the wirilda, *A. retinoides*. They need protection from early frost and the opportunity to ripen their wood well in the summer to encourage flowering.

The vigorous *A. dealbata* is the mimosa found so frequently in florists with its finely divided silvery leaves and fluffy fragrant yellow flowers. The flowers are very welcome in late winter and early spring. It's the toughest of all and although usually tipped by frost or even cut down to the ground, often shoots again from below ground level. It's easily raised from seed, too.

A. retinoides is less strong growing, though still fairly vigorous, and has rather coarser green leaves but similar fragrant flowers which appear first in early spring and then intermittently for the rest of the summer. Of all the acacias this is the most tolerant of chalky soils. z8

Butterfly bush (Buddleia) Now some buddleias, especially the familiar *B. davidii* and its various hybrids, are fairly tough but there are a number of others which need a little shelter and a little more sun to thrive. Three stand out as especially worth growing: *B. fallowiana*, *B. crispa* and *B. colvilei*.

B. fallowiana is a vigorous shrub with white felted foliage and is usually found in its white variety. I grow the natural pale lilac-flowered version and find that this colour melts in with the foliage beautifully. The scent is wonderful and the flowers appear for longer than those of more familiar types in spikes up to 12in (30cm) long. It is liable to be cut down by frost, but in my garden came through unscathed last winter after a low of 3F (−16C). If it's cut back hard it often breaks well from the base and such is its powerful growth that it flowers again the same year.

B. crispa has rather shorter, fatter spikes in lilac with a white eye and a good scent. The branches and shoots are white with down and

The long-flowering evergreen, Carpenteria californica, *is a delightful shrub needing the protection of a sunny wall.*

the whole plant can get quite large after a few mild winters unless pruned in spring.

B. colvilei is altogether different. It can reach a very large size, up to 30–40ft (9–12m), and in its wild home in the Himalayas makes a small tree. The foliage is without the white down of the other two species except in the early stages, turning to a dark glossy green. The individual flowers are larger than those of any other buddleia and come in hanging clusters in June. They are, for a buddleia, an astonishing shade of crimson with a white eye. The younger plants are more tender than mature specimens but all need a warm, dry summer to ripen the wood well and promote flowering. z8

Carpenteria californica A beautiful evergreen shrub with large, fragrant white flowers in small groups at the tips of the leathery evergreen shoots. A real gem for sunny walls, reaching a good height in sheltered or warm areas and in those closer in climate to its native home it's quite happy as a free standing shrub. In less ideal conditions it makes a rounded plant about 6ft (1.8m) high. z8

Californian lilac (Ceanothus) A popular group of both deciduous and evergreen shrubs, it's the evergreens which especially appreciate a

The most beautiful of all annual climbers is Ipomoea 'Heavenly Blue'

For a quick-growing, long-flowering wall shrub you can hardly beat Fremontodendron 'California Glory'

south facing wall or fence. They tend to be vigorous and quickly make substantial plants given this protection. They prefer a well-drained soil, too. As testament to their vigour I planted a 2ft (60cm) plant of 'Autumnal Blue' (z7) against a south facing fence and by the end of its first summer it had reached 5ft (1.5m). It suffered rather from frost in the winter so it was cut back to about 3ft (90cm) and tidied up whereupon it reached 7ft (2.1m) the next summer and was still flowering at Christmas.

Other varieties worth growing, apart from the especially hardy deep blue 'Autumnal Blue' are 'Gloire de Versailles' which is paler and C. impressus with very small dark foliage and deep blue flowers in spring, but not continuing later.

All can be tidied in April if tipped back in winter or pruned if they are getting out of control. z7

Mexican orange blossom (Choisya ternata) One of my favourite plants which, although seeming quite happy on a north facing wall, after recent winter temperatures of 3F (−16C), flowers there for a very brief time compared with its extended season in a warmer situation. In some years I have seen it with flowers in every month of the year.

It's a glossy evergreen with aromatic foliage making a very rounded hummock and the dense growth makes good cover for nesting birds. Its main burst of fragrant white flowers is in mid spring but on a south wall it then flowers a little less intensely at least until the end of the autumn with a few flowers often still in evidence in the middle of winter — except in the worst winters. Although growing contentedly in other situations a south facing position really brings out the best in this valuable shrub. z8

Lobster claw (Clianthus puniceus) Also going under such names as glory pea and parrot's bill, you will be able to take a good guess at the shape of the large flowers which you may not at first recognise as belonging to the pea family. Not a climber, wires are needed to support the arching growths. Young plants should be pinched to encourage bushiness but little other pruning will be needed except possibly to remove dead shoots in spring. The flowers can be red or white and appear for about two months in late spring. This seems an inherently short-lived plant but new plants are easily raised from seed. z9

Fremontodendron Another Californian plant, there are two species but the most common variety is the hybrid between the two, 'Californian Glory'. This is a vigorous plant with dark leaves, the undersides of which are covered in brown down. The flowers are like huge buttercups about 2½in (6.5cm) across and they appear from early summer until early autumn, later in mild seasons. This is not a long-lived plant and, though it can reach 15ft (4.5m) without too much trouble, it may suddenly die for no apparent reason when seeming to thrive. Young plants set out in spring establish the best and they will flower well in their first year. z8

Also try. . . Abutilon × suntense, Cestrum 'Newellii', Cytisus battan-dieri, Escallonia iveyi, Lippia citriodora

Climbers

Trumpet vine (Campsis) Vigorous and exotic self clinging climbers which are at their best in good autumns. The flowers, which appear in late summer and autumn, are like flattened trumpets and come in various shades from yellow through orange to red. C. × *tagliabuana* 'Madame Galen' is the most often seen and is red with orange streaks. The soil must not be allowed to dry out too much in summer so thoughtful watering and timely mulching are best considered if drought threatens. Various forms of C. *radicans*, one of the parents of 'Madame Galen', are sometimes seen with yellow or scarlet flowers. All are appealingly exotic plants but because of their climbing habit and late flowering the flowers are often produced inconveniently high on the plant. z4

Cobaea scandens A perennial climber usually treated as an annual and raised from seed each year. It reaches 6–9ft (1.8–2.7m) in its first year but the roots don't survive the frost outside. It climbs by means of tendrils on the ends of the divided leaves and the large open, trumpet-like flowers open in pale green and gradually age to purple. There is also a white form and another, 'Variegata', with cream markings on the foliage but this must be raised from cuttings and overwintered. Seed is easy to raise if sown in individual peat pots in spring in about 70F (21C); the young plants should be pinched out more than once to encourage bushiness.

A few plants can rapidly cover an area of trellis making an attractive flowering screen, but it's on a fence or wall that the most flowers will be produced. z9

Chilean glory vine (Eccremocarpus scaber) Another one of my favourite climbers and one which really gives its best on a sunny wall or fence. This, too, is often treated as a half-hardy annual and is very easy to raise from seed, but I find that in eastern England it overwinters happily in most years. I've often had it in flower in April after most of the growth has survived the winter. Flowering well into the autumn is to some extent dependent on dead-heading to prevent the formation of the fat seed pods. Leave the pods on and self-sown seedlings may well appear. Grown from seed it makes 4–5ft (1.2–1.5m) in its first year and half as much again the year after. Like *Cobaea* it climbs by means of tendrils on the leaves and the flowers come in loose, pendulous, curling clusters, each flower long and tubular. The commonest colour is orangey red, but yellow and red forms are also available and there are two mixtures, 'Anglia Hybrids' and 'Fireworks' each with a range of five colours. z8

Morning glory (Ipomoea)   Wonderful twining climbers resembling bindweed with the extra elegance of flowers in a range of colours and without the pernicious perennial roots. Raised from seed as half-hardy annuals, high temperatures are needed to ensure prompt germination. It's important to harden off the plants well before setting them out or they may languish for some time. 'Heavenly Blue' is just that and one of the most lovely of all plants with soft, sky blue, open trumpets; 'Scarlet O'Hara' is bright red; while 'Flying Saucers' is soft blue streaked with white. I. purpurea is available as a mixture of mainly darker colours including purple, indigo and maroon.

Passion flower (Passiflora) Most people know the extraordinary floral pattern of the passion flower and although there are over 500 different species only P. caerulea is hardy enough to be widely grown. Although needing cosseting for its first year or two it will then romp away merrily but is still not to be recommended for colder areas. Passion flowers make substantial plants climbing by means of tendrils to make a dense mass of untidy growth.

The intricate flowers appear in summer and are followed by egg-shaped fruits which in hot seasons ripen to a lovely orange shade. At this stage the pulp in which the seed is found is edible and very refreshing. The passion fruits in the shops are usually from a different, less hardy species, P. edulis. z8

Potato vine (Solanum) With one astonishingly beautiful variety and another that's in the top 20 of all climbers, this is an important plant. The pure white-flowered Solanum jasminoides 'Album', always very impressive in the white garden at Sissinghurst, in Kent, is a vigorous climber with loose heads of white flowers all summer. At Sissinghurst it's not grown up a wall and in such situations it's important to take a few cuttings every summer to provide plants to overwinter, just in case. If the plant is against a wall a few cuttings still represent a sensible precaution but in many areas you're more likely to sell the plants at a charity stall than be forced to use them as replacements.

The other variety often grown, S. crispum 'Glasnevin', has more typical potato-style flowers in blue and yellow. Like its white-flowered cousin, it flowers from early summer well into autumn, sometimes still throwing a few flowers in winter. A splendid long flowering plant which thrives on chalk and may well need pruning in spring to keep it within bounds. Its white cousin normally has this job done by the frost. z8

Also try. . . Humulus lupulus 'Aureus', Lonicera 'Dropmore Scarlet', Mutisia ilicifolia, Thunbergia alata, Wisteria sinensis

9

CLAY SOILS

THE PROBLEM

Clay really can be a problem. There's no getting around it with encouraging remarks to turn what seems a problem into an advantage — as I've done in some other chapters. Clay is a problem that needs solving. Clay is heavy, wet, sticky and often totally unworkable; it's cold in spring and it rots delicate plants very efficiently as well as weighing down the gardener's boots so he can hardly move.

But — and I have to say it — there are advantages too. Except in dry summers clay soils don't suffer from drought, they retain a lot of plant foods and can be turned into very fertile soils.

The difficulties come about as a direct result of the composition of the soil. The particles that make up a clay soil are very small indeed, the smallest found in mineral soils. The result is that, unlike the more granular sandy and gravelly soils, they bind together into a cohesive mass helped by the water that they retain in the tiny spaces between the particles.

If you take a jar of grit and add some water very slowly, all that happens is that the water fills up the spaces — you can watch it happen. Even if you stir in the water, there is little in the way of physical change that takes place. When eventually it dries out the grit will still look much the same.

If, on the other hand, you do the same with clay (or flour which behaves in the same way) it looks quite different. If you start with dry clay the water will not even sink in to begin with, it simply rests in droplets on the surface and will need stirring to encourage it to mix. It will then change from a powder to a thick paste and then to a cream as you add more water and stir. Leave it to dry out and it is quite likely to set solid. Unlike sand or grit it changes in form noticeably as water is added and as it dries.

Clay soils behave in a similar way. When very dry they tend to set hard and the rain runs off without soaking in. As the rain does eventually penetrate, the soil becomes sticky and malleable until eventually it turns quite greasy. When it eventually dries out it is likely to set very hard and shrink to leave cracks through which the rain runs without soaking in. At this stage you would expect many plants to wilt and die but, although the soil seems to be bone dry, there is still water being held by the soil particles which the plants can use.

The particular properties of clay soils create problems for the plants and the gardener. So much water is retained in the soil and for so long that plants have to be able to tolerate these damp conditions for long periods, often with little air to help compensate. They also have to be able to tolerate the cracking which develops as they dry.

Clay is a problem for the gardener too, as only when the soil is fairly dry can it be dug or worked in other ways and this means that cultivation is more dependent on the weather than with other soils. Of course this means that improving clay soil is also more difficult as this has to be done at just the right time.

There are advantages though. The fact that clay soils are basically water retentive makes them a good basis for growing many plants if they can be improved to make them more workable. And because of their chemical structure they also retain their plant foods for much longer than other soils, so that plants can use them before they are leached away by rain. Fertiliser applications are not wasted and the nutrients released by organic matter as it rots are used efficiently.

Clay soils can be acid or alkaline so a soil test is helpful if the plants in neighbouring gardens don't give you a clue; but they are also more stable in their acidity and alkalinity and less easy to change.

ALLEVIATING THE PROBLEM

There are a number of ways that the problem of clay soils can be alleviated and one way it can be solved — by moving house! But assuming that you don't wish to move away there are still ways you can make your soil easier to live with.

The first is to drain the soil. On clay soils it's often easier to drain only the surface layers than to attempt a full scale drainage operation and systems to achieve this are now available. But drainage is only part of the solution. It's all very well to have the means in place by which surplus water can be conducted away to a drain or soakaway but if the soil is still hanging on to it, there is little point. So the soil itself needs attention, too.

Digging is the first thing to think about but not necessarily the first thing to actually do! On a clay soil digging is a long and arduous job and needs to be started early in the autumn if you are to do a reasonable amount in any one season without ending up in hospital. This is especially true as I have to confess that I'm going to recommend

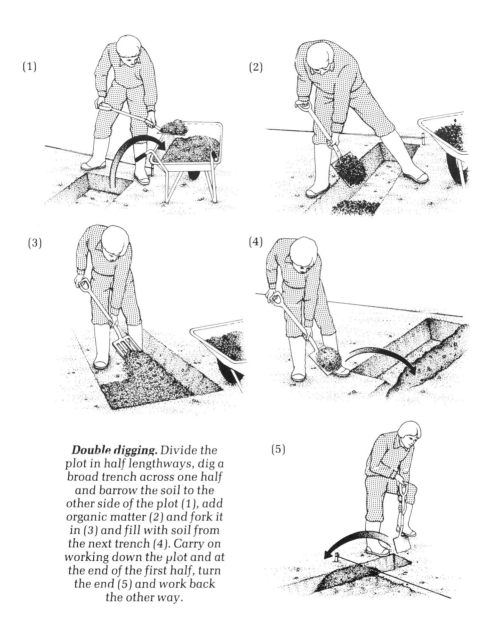

(1)

(2)

(3)

(4)

Double digging. *Divide the plot in half lengthways, dig a broad trench across one half and barrow the soil to the other side of the plot (1), add organic matter (2) and fork it in (3) and fill with soil from the next trench (4). Carry on working down the plot and at the end of the first half, turn the end (5) and work back the other way.*

(5)

old fashioned double digging if you want to do the job properly. This involves not only turning over the top spit but the lower one too. Even in an established garden this may never have been done and the lower level will be very hard and compact, not to say infertile, too.

When you start to dig you may well find that below about one spade's depth the soil deteriorates noticeably owing to lack of aeration and cultivation and it's important to ensure that this poor subsoil is not mixed with the more fertile topsoil during digging. It's also important to start the job when the soil is reasonably dry, and to curb your understandable enthusiasm for this delightful occupation when the soil is wet.

At this point you are doubtless expecting me to suggest that you add more organic matter than you've ever seen in your life before. Well, you're getting the right idea and this will be very helpful. As you're going to be using a fair amount, this organic matter had better be the cheapest available and so spent mushroom compost or peat bought in bulk is probably the most convenient unless of course you have been making large quantities of your own compost.

If the soil is not too wet or rock hard you will be able to fork your organic matter into the bottom layer — which is far more effective than spreading it in a layer on the forked soil. This does depend on the organic matter being fairly friable too — peat is ideal in this respect as is mushroom compost. It's always suggested that the top layer be left rough for winter frosts to help break down and notwithstanding the scepticism of many this does actually happen. So if you can improve the subsoil as you dig in the autumn and early winter, then leave it rough over the winter and in spring fork more organic matter into the topsoil, you'll have the ideal thorough preparation.

'But what about grit?' I hear you cry. This can help, too, and if you want to do the job properly it can be forked into both layers at the appropriate stage with the organic matter — in effect creating a border of potting compost. But please make sure you use grit and not builders' sand which is quite useless by comparison.

You will find that adding all this material often increases the height of borders and to reduce this accumulation you may need to remove some of the subsoil whilst digging. The other alternative is to raise the beds slightly and this can have a very beneficial effect on the drainage and give you the opportunity to create a special soil mix for the top

Raised beds can be used to grow susceptible plants on badly drained or limy sites. Bond the blocks of stone or peat and plant in the cracks.

layer. This is likely to be the only way of growing plants needing free drainage, like alpines, on clay soil.

Some soils are so sticky that they are very difficult to dig and, of course, many gardeners don't have the inclination or, like me, the fitness to do a great deal of heavy digging so in such circumstances another approach is necessary. Organic matter spread on the surface can, over the years, have a very beneficial effect and peat, mushroom compost, garden compost, bark and other materials have been used successfully. They are simply spread on the surface in spring when the soil is moist, left in place all summer and forked into the surface in the autumn to be replaced by another layer. This method can be used in conjunction with chemical soil improvers.

As well as organic matter and grit there are chemical materials that can be added to clay soils to improve them. Lime is the most commonly used and can be very helpful. It works by chemically encouraging the soil particles to gather together into groups — flocculate is the technical term — to make larger particles or crumbs. These have larger spaces between them through which air can circulate and water drain away. Lime works well but whether you use it depends largely on the existing pH level of your soil and on the plants you want to grow. If your soil is acid and you want to keep it that way then using lime would be a mistake as it would if your clay soil is already fairly limy.

Many branded clay curing products are available and the one thing they have in common is that they're expensive and if they work at all it's only for a limited period. Generally you would be far better off spending the same amount of money on a few bags of organic matter or on paying someone to do the digging for you. But in a small garden where other methods are more difficult to apply these products can be useful. I suggest that you buy just one pack and try it out before lashing out on too much.

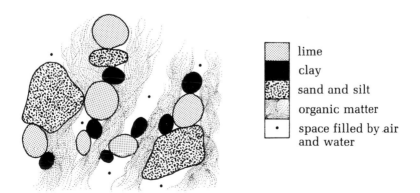

lime
clay
sand and silt
organic matter
space filled by air and water

Clay and lime both have the effect of binding together particles of clay soil to let water drain through more effectively.

SOLVING THE PROBLEM WITH PLANTS

Trees

Horse chestnut (Aesculus) As I look out of my window there are three large horse chestnut trees in the school grounds that border the garden. They're stunning when they flower in spring. But they all flower at slightly different times and the flower spikes on one are more impressive than those on the others. All were doubtless raised from conkers and the natural variation is coming out. So if you want a horse chestnut buy a named variety.

The Indian horse chestnut is especially impressive and the best of these is undoubtedly *A. indica* 'Sydney Pearce' (z7) with long flower spikes in white with yellow markings and a pink tint. If small boys insistently throwing sticks, or worse, to knock down conkers worries you then plant *A. hippocastanum* 'Beaumannii' (z4) with double white flowers which are sterile and so set no nuts.

These are very substantial trees but for something a little smaller try the red buckeye, *A. pavia* (z5), with crimson flowers or *A.* × *mutabilis* (z5) which is sometimes little more than a large shrub with red and yellow flowers.

Flowering crab apples (Malus) Excellent small garden trees, the crab apples give you at least two seasons of display with the flowers in spring and the fruits in the autumn. Generally they make small- to medium-sized trees, sometimes with rather tangled growth and have the excellent capacity to pollinate fruiting apples while serving their decorative purpose.

'John Downie' is universally regarded as the most impressive variety with white flowers and big slightly conical fruits coloured orange with paler streaks on trees with a conveniently upright habit. On top of its other advantages the large fruits also make good crab apple jelly. 'Golden Hornet' has bright yellow fruits which are less edible but last well and although the tree spreads in the end it starts off with fairly compact growth.

My favourite, I have to say, is *M.* × *robusta* in its red form and this makes a noticeably spreading tree with pinkish flowers and scarlet fruits which seem to be left till the last of all by marauding birds. The mass of red apples amongst the twiggy branches is most pleasing on a cold sunny winter's day. z4

Ostrya Sometimes known as the hop hornbeams or ironwoods, these are closely related to the more familiar hornbeam and are similarly subtle in their appeal. Catkins in the spring, hop-like fruits later in the year and yellow autumn colour combined with an attractive shape make them very appealing in a restrained way.

The American ironwood, *O. virginiana* (z5), seems to be least cultivated in spite of its attractive pyramidal form and good autumn colour. *O. carpinifolia* (z6) is seen more often and I especially like its spring catkins and the hop-like fruits which are about 2in (5cm) long. The only other one seen is *O. japonica* (z6) which seems to be especially generous with its fruits.

Also try. . . Fraxinus species, *Prunus* species, *Tilia* species

Hedges

Prunus × cistena Sometimes described in books as the purple-leaf sand cherry, most people know it simply as 'Cistena'. It's a naturally dwarf plant with white flowers set against rich, purplish red foliage which retains its colour all season. Later in the season there are black fruits, too. Only one clipping a year is needed after flowering although this will inevitably mean a loss of berries. z2

Roses (Rosa) Wonderful plants for flowering hedges, if I had the space I'd plant a whole hedge of 'Penelope' (z6) straight away even if the garden didn't need a hedge at all, just for the simple pleasure of looking at it and smelling it. 'Penelope' is a semi-double soft pink, repeat flowering Hybrid Musk rose which reaches 5ft (1.5m) in height. 'Felicia' (z6) is another Hybrid Musk of about the same size but with more apricot coloured flowers.

'Queen Elizabeth' (z6), that rather uncharacteristic floribunda, can reach the same size with no trouble at all but is of such upright habit that in spite of its being recommended for a hedge for many years I find it always looks rather gangly and inelegant.

The various varieties of *Rosa rugosa* (z2) make excellent tough hedges which can be pruned severely in spring if necessary or left to make a stout impenetrable barrier. The flowers are big and the hips big, too. 'Roseraie de l'Hay' in red is the most often seen though there are white and pink types too.

For a smaller hedge the white floribunda 'Iceberg' (z6) is very good — as long as you spray against mildew regularly. The foliage is pale and fresh and the slight pink tint to the bud soon fades to a pure white flower. One of the best of all roses, in spite of its mildew, and an excellent long flowering hedge. The newer white 'Margaret Merrill' (z6), with much darker foliage, is now also being recommended as a hedge but on my gravelly soil I find it rather less robust. On clay it should thrive.

Laurustinus (Viburnum tinus) A very valuable winter flowering evergreen, ideal for an informal hedge although I have also seen it clipped more neatly. The leaves are dark and usually glossy, the buds pink and the white flowers are carried in flat heads. The flowers

Eranthis × tubergeniana 'Guinea Gold', a choicer version of the winter aconite, is a little more delicate, but more expensive.

appear in winter and sometimes there are dark blue fruits later. My favourite is the variety 'Gwenllian' with darker buds, slightly pink tinged flowers and a flowering and fruiting capacity better than all the others. It tolerates shade and salt spray as well as heavy soil. One of the few essential garden shrubs and definitely worth using as a hedge. For a slower growing hedge the variety 'Eve Price' is similar but smaller in leaf and growth. z7

Also try. . . Carpinus betulus, Berberis species, Prunus laurocerasus

Shrubs

Abelia Amongst the best of small garden shrubs, making up in charm for the lack of punch in the flowers, it thrives in a sunny situation and although occasionally rumoured to be delicate seems to me to be perfectly tough. *A. × grandiflora* is a partially evergreen shrub, retaining just some leaves, with a long succession of pink and white flowers from summer onwards. It makes a neat, rounded bush — though not a horrid hummock — and is ideal for using as an occasional larger plant at the front of a border.

There is also a variegated form, 'Francis Mason', which has leaves softly marked in golden green making it one of the more subtle variegated shrubs. Altogether a very valuable plant. z6

Angelica tree (Aralia elata) Grown for its huge foliage these relations

The new crocosmias like this 'Lucifer' with their larger flowers and longer flowering are a great improvement on the older varieties.

of the ivies make large suckering shrubs. They are vigorous growers with spiny stems carrying massive doubly divided leaves up to 5ft (1.5m) long held more or less horizontally at the ends of the stems. As if the big glossy foliage is not enough there are also the flowers, which are small and white but carried in large heads. There are two variegated forms but they are rarely available. z3

Mexican orange blossom (Choisya ternata) One of my favourite shrubs, its glossy, fingered, evergreen foliage is slightly aromatic. It forms a rounded plant which, if planted in the sun, is covered in heads of sweetly scented white flowers from spring to autumn and occasionally in winter in warmer, sheltered spots.

There is a recently introduced yellow leaved version, 'Sundance', which has been heavily promoted but my only experience of it is its death from frost in its first winter in the garden. Notwithstanding the undoubted beauty of *Philadelphus coronarius* 'Aureus' I remain sceptical about the appeal of yellow foliage and white flowers. z8

Forsythia If this plant was difficult to grow gardeners everywhere would be clamouring to try it but as it is, like aubrieta, it's viewed with a little disdain. Ignore the snobs and look for yourself, it's a wonderful plant and if you get the variety 'Lynwood' which usually produces the most colourful display, you'll never regret it. The flowers of 'Lynwood' are an especially rich shade of yellow but if you prefer something a little paler try 'Primulina'. Other good varieties to look out for are 'Beatrix Farrand', an upright type with probably the largest flowers and the vigorous 'Karl Sax'. The problem is that after flowering they are undoubtedly rather dull but benefit from a clematis or other climber trained through them. z5

Witch hazel (Hamamelis) Another of my favourites the scent of these winter-flowering shrubs is simply captivating. In competition with a bowl of hyacinths in a cool room a branch of witch hazel wins hands down. Mind you, cutting branches from witch hazels is only for the lucky few who have a number of large plants which can spare them.

Witch hazels are expensive to buy and slow growing so choose carefully. *H. mollis* 'Pallida' (z5) is the one most widely available and a good plant too with large sulphury flowers and a lovely scent. If you prefer a different colour, *H.* × *intermedia* 'Jelena' (z4), is yellow but tinted slightly with coppery red and the flowers are large and carried in generous numbers, too. This is my second choice these days especially as its autumn colours in reds, oranges and yellows are more flamboyant than those of other varieties — though all are good.

One more you might like to consider is *H. japonica* 'Arborea' (z5). This can even make a small tree rather than just a shrub and its characteristic flat sprays of branches make it a very unusual and attractive plant.

Pieris floribunda On heavy clay soils a fair amount of improvement is often needed to get the best out of pieris but this species is that little bit tougher than most. It lacks the flamboyant red shoots of some of the other types but I feel that the flower spikes, which in the variety 'Elongata' are especially long, are more elegant. They are also branched rather attractively. z5

Rose (Rosa) Roses hardly need describing they are so universally popular so I can only recommend some favourites.

One group which I'm always surprised not to see more often in garden centres is the English Roses bred in Staffordshire by David Austin. These are best described as 'new old roses', roses with flowers like old fashioned shrub roses but with the capacity to flower all summer like modern varieties. 'Graham Rose' is rich yellow, 'Mary Rose' is pink, 'Fair Bianca' is white and there are plenty more. Look out for them.

The genuine shrub roses are becoming more and more popular and of the vast number available it's difficult to pick out just a few. So, all I'll say is that you can see hybrid teas and floribundas in any garden but old roses are less common, more interesting, often more strongly scented and have altogether more character. Go and see some and then choose. z6

Lilac (Syringa) Another wonderfully scented shrub and, whereas I was being very cautious about cutting branches of witch hazel to bring into the house, cutting lilac is a different matter. The fact is that the shrubs themselves are less than attractive, being tall and rather gangly with dull foliage. Of course when they're at their best they look and smell wonderful but it's for such a short time that it seems to me that siting the plants away from the house and cutting the flowers and bringing them indoors where they can be better appreciated is perhaps a wise counsel.

As to varieties to choose, well, there are a great many and they do vary a little in their flowering time so it's possible to choose them to get a slight spread of flowering but it will still only cover about six weeks over the earlies, mid-seasons and lates. The sky blue 'Firmament' is early, the white 'Madame Lemoine' is a mid season variety and the purple 'Charles Jolly' is one of the latest. z3

Viburnum plicatum In its variety 'Mariesii' this is one of the most stunning of shrubs when in flower. It's best placed in a part of the garden where visitors will come on it by surprise as the effect will then be even more dramatic.

There are two main reasons why this shrub creates such impact. First of all there's the striking horizontal arrangement of the branches creating a tiered effect. And capitalising on this usual feature the lacecap style flower clusters stand up in a double row from the leaf joints all the way along. This is a medium-sized shrub and not a quick growing one which needs space to show off its good looks to the best advantage. z4

Also try... Corylus avellana, Cotinus coggygria, Philadelphus varieties, Senecio 'Sunshine', Weigela varieties

Perennials

Wood anemone (Anemone nemorosa) An adaptable plant, the wood anemone grows well on all but the wettest clay soils. In Britain it grows wild in woods all over the country and this is typical of its adaptability. All it needs is shade and preferably for the top few inches to be improved a little and it's perfectly happy. It grows only a few inches high and flowers in early spring, its many petalled heads bobbing in the breeze followed quickly by ferny foliage. Its flowers are a real delight at a time when we're looking for something cheerful and are usually white although even in the wild they can be tinged with pink. There are a number of named varieties, such as 'Robinsoniana', with large lavender flowers. z4

Michaelmas daisies (Aster) This is a large group, the common name of which should strictly only be applied to *A. novi-belgii*. Many suffer shamefully from mildew but this is less of a problem in water retentive soil and where the air doesn't get too dry. However, there are varieties that are relatively resistant particularly amongst the dwarfer types.

Outstanding is *Aster × frikartii* 'Monch' (z6). It flowers from July to October with blooms of blue with a tint of lilac on neat, self-supporting plants and has no mildew. The plantsman Graham Thomas describes it as 'one of the six best plants and should be in every garden'!

The varieties of *A. amellus* (z5) are all worth considering for their neatness and healthy growth but for a trouble free traditional Michaelmas daisy, try 'Climax', one of the oldest varieties, but still one of the best. It's a big plant, reaching 6ft (1.8m), with blue flowers in autumn. For a colour that is impossible to place with any other try the huge flowered 'Alma Potschke' in salmon tinged with rose pink. Half shade or full sun suits them all.

Camassia leichtlinii There are a number of bulbs which in spite of being easy to grow are not well known and this is one of them. The bulbs themselves can get very large and in early summer they produce narrow flowering spikes up to 4ft (1.2m) in height studded with starry blue flowers. This plant grows wild from the Sierra Nevada in the south to Vancouver in the north of the American continent and there are a number of wild variants which have led to a range of cultivated varieties. Most are in shades of blue but there is also a slightly creamy variety with double flowers known as 'Plena'.

They are all happy in a heavy, damp soil in sun or a little shade but the more the soil is improved the better the flower spikes will be. z5

Montbretia (Crocosmia) Recently introduced hybrids have transformed the image of the familiar montbretia into that of a sought after garden plant. They have larger flowers, better displayed in a range of shades, and are altogether most excellent plants. They are best in improved clay soils rather than the original clay but will then spread well and flower beautifully.

All have green, grassy or iris-like foliage although there are one or two varieties like the apricot-flowered 'Soltfare' with bronzed leaves to be found and more are currently under trial.

A number of the best of the modern hybrids were raised at Bressingham Gardens in Norfolk and of these 'Lucifer' is the one which is the most popular — and deservedly so. Its flowers are a brilliant flame red and the strong growing plants reach 3½ft (1m). Others worth growing are the rather shorter 'Firebird' with rich orange flowers and 'Spitfire' in a brighter orange which is shorter still. z7

Winter aconite (Eranthis hyemalis) Related to the hellebores, the winter aconite is a delightful winter carpeter flowering very early in the season with big buttercup-like flowers over a ruff of green leaves. Once settled down they naturalise well and make a wonderful start to

White foxgloves will seed themselves on heavy soils although occasional purple plants will probably continue to appear.

the year with snowdrops and other bulbs to follow. By mid summer all trace has gone. Unaccountably they sometimes refuse to settle; tubers may simply fail to sprout, usually because they've become too dry before planting, or eventually one or two flower happily but never spread. They're worth persevering with as they will usually settle in the end.

There is a larger-flowered plant with slightly purple tinted foliage called *E.* × *tubergeniana* 'Guinea Gold' which is rather expensive but worth growing, although it does not seem to naturalise so well. z5

Helenium Yellow dominates the late summer garden and more often than not the heleniums provide it. But these rather brash members of the daisy family have more than just yellow to boast about with reds and mahoganies, too. They are all robust plants, not to say invasive, which will muscle aside less assertive neighbours and they flower in summer and early autumn. 'Riverton Beauty' is a good yellow, 'Crimson Beauty' is mahogany brown and 'Moerheim Beauty' is the closest to red. Heights vary from 3–5ft (0.9–1.5m) and they're all best in sunshine. z3

Inula If you like big yellow daisies that are showy and have poise without being coarse and vulgar then *I. magnifica* (z5) is the plant for you. There's no doubt it's a big plant, reaching 6ft (1.8m) with no trouble at all and it has foliage to match so it needs a fair amount of space. And on top of the lot come huge yellow daisies up to 6in (15cm) across. Stately I suppose is the word for it. Faint hearts should go for the British native elecampane, *I. helenium* (z5), instead which is a smaller version and although very attractive in itself doesn't quite have the appeal of its big brother.

Daffodils (Narcissus) Now, everyone knows daffodils and there's hardly a half serious gardener in the country who doesn't nurture and enjoy at least one clump. And they're ideal spring bulbs for improved clay soils. If you plant them in pure clay then you could have problems as they may well rot, but with the sort of improvements suggested earlier, even over a small area, they will thrive mightily.

Recommending particular varieties can be rather fruitless as there are so many good ones to be had. So, as usual in such circumstances, I will simply praise my own favourites and leave it to you as to whether or not you agree.

'Tête à Tête' is a small plant with a long trumpet and two or sometimes three flowers on a stem. It doesn't always establish well or increase speedily but is a real charmer in such a clear yellow that it's irresistible — it's somehow dainty and robust at the same time. And unlike some of the more choice types it's not expensive which is good news.

The long narrow trumpet is a characteristic which comes from *Narcissus cyclamineus*, itself well worth growing and good naturalised in grass. The characteristics of this species also turn up in a number of taller early flowering varieties — the pure yellow 'February Gold' which rarely flowers when its name suggests; 'Jack Snipe' which is creamy with a pale yellow cup; and 'Beryl', yellow with an orange cup.

For naturalising on clay there are two species that are especially suitable. *N. cyclamineus* is a dainty plant with strongly reflexed petals like a cyclamen which will increase well when happy and *N. bulbocodium*, the hoop petticoat daffodil, with its large open trumpet, will even seed itself.

In the more traditional form 'Fortune' is probably the best of the big yellow daffs, 'Mount Hood' is a white version and 'Geranium' is a good white with an orange cup in the 'narcissus' vein. All are worth naturalising in rough grass or growing in clumps in borders. z5

Jacob's ladder (Polemonium) Bright, finely cut foliage stands as a base for erect spikes of clear blue flowers, each with an eye of yellow anthers. The plants reach 2–3ft (60–90cm) high and, if dead-headed regularly, flower from spring for many weeks. P. caeruleum (z3) is the usual one seen and there is a white version too, but P. foliosissimum (z4) with darker, more purplish flowers which appear a little later is also worth looking out for. It grows rather taller, too.

Rodgersia Heavy border soil is needed for these impressive plants with their handsome foliage in many forms. They grow in damp places by the waterside too; but in beds and borders where something rather opulent and slightly exotic is needed that won't grow too big, rodgersias are ideal.

I like R. pinnata 'Superba' (z4) the best with its leaves divided like those of a rose though on a much grander scale. They're slightly furrowed and a delicious bronzy purple colour and this combines beautifully with their fluffy pink heads of flowers. R. aesculifolia (z4) has green leaves like those of a horse chestnut tree and creamy or sometimes pink flowers and R. podophylla (z4) has similar foliage though slightly jagged in outline. In this case the flowers are beige.

Finally, there's R. tabularis (z5) with round green leaves whose stem is attached in the middle, rather like plates spinning on canes. All grow to 3–4ft (0.9–1.2m).

Also try. . . Anemone hybrida, Podophyllum emodi, Prunella web-
biana, Solidago varieties

Annuals and Biennials

Love-lies-bleeding (Amaranthus caudatus) Improved clay for this one certainly, but what a wonderful plant — with only one slight drawback. A hardy annual in most areas, the great joy of this plant is its long red millet-like tassels which hang down from plants up to 4ft (1.2m) high, sometimes swishing the ground. The tassels dry well and there is a good green version, too, called 'Viridis'. I've grown both in big tubs and very impressive they are too, but they are at their best with a good root run in borders of rich soil where they make wonderful plants.

There are a number of other varieties, like 'Red Fox', with especially dark foliage and upright rather than dangling flower spikes but I find they need slightly better treatment. The coloured leaf forms are altogether more fussy.

The drawback is that A. caudatus self-sows very generously — too generously as you usually only need about three plants and are liable to be blessed with hundreds but a sweep through with the hoe will sort them out.

Foxglove (Digitalis purpurea) The foxglove is a biennial or short-lived perennial which in the wild has purple flowers each with a pretty speckled throat. It's a lovely plant for slightly shaded spots in the wild garden. I have a great affection for the white version, but at the moment seem to have acquired a white form without spots which is a disappointing creature when compared to a good white with purple spots in the throat.

There are a number of varieties which vary to a greater or lesser degree from the wild type in height, the arrangement of the flowers and colour. 'Foxy' is short, comes in many colours and has flowers all round the stem. The 'Excelsior Hybrids' are up to 5ft (1.5m) tall with the flowers held more or less horizontally so that they can be seen more easily. Both are more colourful but lack charm. They will all seed themselves if left to get on with it, but there's no telling what you'll get unless you stick to just one colour.

Sunflower (Helianthus) Not only is the sunflower a happy plant on clay soils but it's a useful one, too. If you grow the taller types the root system is equally extensive and strikes deep into the soil. When the plant dies the roots rot and leave tunnels down through the soil which help carry away surplus water.

If you or your children want to grow real whoppers then 'Russian Giant' is the one to try. Seed sold for birds often produces respectable plants and there are a number of tall varieties with flowers in a mixture of yellow and russett shades, not just the yellow. There's also a dwarf fully double one, 'Teddy Bear', which some people like but which I find difficult to recommend except for its entertainment value.

Mignonette (Reseda odorata) One of the sweetest smelling of annuals though not one of the more showy. As long as the top few inches of soil are improved and it doesn't lie too wet for too long, this plant will succeed. It can be sown where it is to flower or raised in pots and planted out where it will sprawl prettily and carry its green flowers with red tints for many weeks. It's always worth having a few plants, especially by a path.

Also try... Limnanthes *douglasii,* Tagetes *signata varieties,* Zea *mays*

10

CHALKY SOILS

THE PROBLEM

Considering the continuing elitism that infects some people who garden on acid soils, this chapter is a strong plea for the treatment of lime loving plants as the equal of acid lovers in terms of beauty and elegance. Why should those who can grow rhododendrons and the many lovely shrubs in the same family, plus the wide range of other plants needing similar soil, think their gardens are so special? Look dispassionately on acid loving and lime loving plants and you'll find it hard to say that one group is intrinsically superior to the other.

But first let's clear up a confusion about the two terms which describe plants' taste in soil — calcifuge and calcicole. Calcifuge plants are those that like acid soils. The level of acidity is expressed as a pH number. Acid soils have a pH below 7, 7 is neutral and alkaline soils are above 7. Calcicole plants are those that like an alkaline soil, above pH7. An easy way to remember it, which my Mum invented, is to notice that there are two *l*s in ca*l*cico*l*e and they stand for *l*ime *l*oving — simple.

One particular type of alkaline soil creates the most serious problem and that's a shallow soil overlying solid chalk or limestone. There are some parts of the UK where gardens of this sort are common and they bring their own unique difficulties. But a hint of their promise can be seen from a look at the British native flora which grows in such conditions — there's a range of attractive trees and shrubs like whitebeams, viburnums, clematis and honeysuckle plus a wonderfully rich ground flora. This includes many grasses, orchids, cowslips, thymes, pulsatillas, rock roses. . . the list is a long one.

Gardens made up of a shallow layer of soil over solid chalk or limestone have a number of inherent features which make them difficult to cultivate. The first is simply the physical presence of so much rock, so near the surface of the soil. This makes it almost

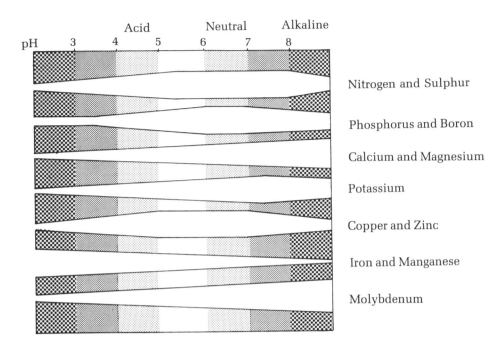

The availability of plant foods varies according to the acidity and alkalinity of the soil.

impossible to make a good sized planting hole without the help of a pick axe and putting up a fence or supports for raspberries or sweet peas becomes a major operation. There's almost no soil in the sense that most of us use the term and for many plants this has to be created by the gardener.

Next there's drought. Water may not drain through at once, puddles may even form for a short time, but very quickly the surface soil and then the upper layers of rock become extremely dry — although some plants will force their roots down through the rock and eventually build an extensive root system. There is another, more positive, side to this and that is that cultivation is usually possible quite soon after rain whereas on other soils it would need to be delayed for some time.

There is also the problem of nutrient deficiencies referred to in Chapter 13 on acid soils. At a pH of about 7.5, potash and manganese become much less available and the availability to plants of phosphate, iron and boron starts to decline, too, so that above pH8 all are in short supply. The amount of nitrogen available can also be reduced, not so much by the high pH as by the constant leaching due to the rapid drainage. All this can leave the soil very impoverished indeed.

Added to this is that in alkaline soils organic matter breaks down quickly as bacteriological action is greatly enhanced by the high pH. So water retention is not improved as it might be on other soils and the reservoir of nutrients that organic matter usually provides is relatively short-lived.

Another difficulty is the poor root anchorage of trees whose roots are unable to penetrate the rock and indeed some trees like beech (*Fagus sylvatica*), which grows on shallow, chalky soil, naturally produce a broad but shallow root system.

ALLEVIATING THE PROBLEM

There's not much to be done about solid rock — it can't be spirited away. But, as many writers have done before, I can quote the garden created by Sir Frederick Stern at Highdown in Sussex which was made in an old chalk pit and in which there was virtually no soil at all before the garden was made. Here a wonderful range of plants was grown and this achievement should be an inspiration to anyone gardening in such a situation.

The aim of cultivation on soil overlying chalk should be to increase the depth of soil available into which plants can root, to encourage the soil to retain as much water as possible, to reduce the alkalinity — at least a little — and to ensure that all plant foods are freely available.

At times the pickaxe will be a necessary garden tool for excavating planting holes. Liberal quantities of organic matter can be added to these holes which will provide the sites for trees, shrubs and other larger plants. Smaller plants can go around them at the edge of the excavations.

Mulching helps increase the depth of good soil without the need to break up the chalk over the whole garden, although if it can be loosened this will aid root penetration to lower layers. Leaf mould in particular is frequently recommended by gardeners on chalk. Some

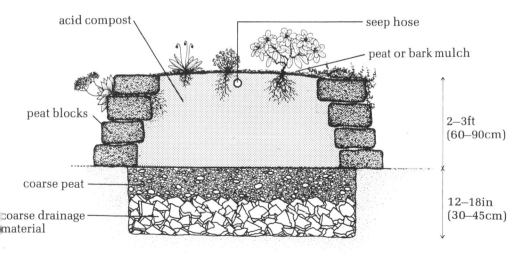

Constructing a peat bed out of peat blocks with special compost and added drainage.

Limy soils grow wonderful plants of Kolkwitzia amabilis *which produces its delightful pink and white flowers in early summer.*

even say that it should be applied each year in spring and autumn, such is the humus hunger of such soils that it's rapidly devoured. Peat will last the longest and also help reduce the alkalinity a little. If bought in the largest bales, usually 300 litres, or ordered in bulk for delivery by lorry, it's relatively economical. But almost any organic matter will do.

As well as improving the topsoil the addition of organic matter to excavated areas will greatly increase its water holding capacity. The alternative is to water in summer, and this may still be unavoidable. So in the early stages it will pay to install an outside water tap and, in larger gardens, a permanent network of pipes. As it may not be practical to bury them to protect them against frost, they should be drained in winter to avoid bursts.

Reducing the alkalinity is a sensible goal though one which is unlikely to be achieved with any great degree of success. Acid reacting fertilisers such as sulphate of ammonia can be used and alkaline ones such as bonemeal avoided. Organic matter such as spent mushroom compost, which is usually very limy, can also be avoided. This will not only help broaden the range of plants which can be grown but will

One of the most popular of trees is this yellow-leaved Robinia pseudacacia 'Frisia' which does well on both chalky and stony soils if well fed.

also help prevent some nutrient deficiencies which may otherwise be a problem.

As mentioned earlier a variety of deficiencies can occur but the generous dressings of organic matter, especially well rotted farmyard or horse manure which are especially rich in minor plant foods, will help counteract this tendency. But there will often be a need for supplementary feeding and a tonic of sequestered trace elements, now widely available, will usually provide all that the plants need if given once or twice a year.

SOLVING THE PROBLEM WITH PLANTS

Trees

Ash (Fraxinus excelsior) In Britain the ash forms woods on chalk soils, especially in wetter areas, and also grows with oaks. Its natural home extends right across Europe and north Africa and into Asia. It makes a large and shapely tree but is often seen in gardens in its weeping form, 'Pendula'. This makes large rounded mounds of branches which hang down vertically, often rubbing the ground. It's usually grafted on to a straight stem of the ordinary ash and may get little taller than the height of this stem unless trained higher. Stakes and canes can be used to continue vertical growth before allowing the tree to weep. Occasionally trees are seen which weep from very high up and these are usually grafted on to mature ash trees, sometimes as high as 30ft (9m) from the ground. z4

Magnolia kobus A lovely small tree, sometimes trained as a large shrub, which is underused as a garden tree. The one drawback, which for many gardeners is a big one, is that it doesn't flower when young. It often takes ten years to flower and then it starts sparsely and builds up over a few years. But when it finally reaches its best it's a lovely sight with pure white, lightly scented flowers about 4in (10cm) across in spring. A tough and reliable tree if you've the patience to wait for the flowers. z6

Also try. . . Acer campestre, Carpinus betulus, Fagus sylvatica, Malus varieties, Morus nigra

Hedges

Box (Buxus sempervirens) A wonderfully adaptable hedging plant which can be used for dwarf edging hedges no more than 12in (30cm) high, for topiary and for tall formal, garden hedges, too. The knack is to choose different varieties for different purposes. If you want a dwarf hedge the short variety 'Suffruticosa' is the one to go for. For a larger hedge choose the dense growing 'Latifolia', for a tall hedge try 'Handsworthensis' and for a tall screen choose 'Arborescens'. z6

Shrubby cinquefoil (Potentilla) Not often seen as a hedge plant, perhaps because some varieties are rather floppy, the more upright types nevertheless are very effective. Ones to try are the white-flowered 'Farrer's White' and 'Mount Everest', the bright yellow 'Elizabeth' and the primrose 'Katherine Dykes' which is one of the tallest of the group at about 6ft (1.8m). They are all best in sun and need good preparation. z2

Also try. . . Berberis species, Fagus sylvatica, Prunus laurocerasus, Taxus baccata, Thuya plicata

Shrubs

Clematis The best climbers for chalky soils, it's especially important to give their roots the shade so often recommended as they may not be able to penetrate as deeply as they would like in search of their own coolness and moisture. You have a vast selection to choose from to flower in most months of the year. In winter there's the exquisite flowers of *Clematis cirrhosa* var. *balearica* (z7) which are creamy white and nodding so you must look closely to see the delightful reddish spots inside. The ferny foliage is also very attractive. Later there's one of my favourites, *C. macropetala* (z5), a vigorous one, the flowers soft blue with white centres. Next come the large flowered hybrids and you can take your pick of those for the chalk suits them all.

Finally, there's the little group of yellow-flowered varieties typified by *C. orientalis* (z6), *C. tangutica* (z5) and 'Bill McKenzie' (z5). The names in this group are a little confused but they are all good, making very vigorous plants with fleshy orange-yellow flowers in autumn and white fluffy seed heads later.

Daphne There's a common misconception that all daphnes are lime haters but this is not the case; most will do well on chalky soils if fed well. In the UK, *Daphne mezereum* (z5) is naturally a plant of chalk areas. This is a deciduous species flowering in late winter and early spring with upright branches in its youth but becoming more rounded with age. The flowers, carried tight on the branches, are deep rose or white; they have a strong and delicious scent.

Amongst the evergreens there are three which are especially worthy of growing. *D. collina* (z7) is a very attractive small shrub making a dome shaped bush in full sun and in a soil that doesn't dry out. The purple, heavily scented flowers appear in spring. The trailing *D. cneorum* (z5) is another splendid plant for the front of a raised bed. A humus-rich but well-drained soil in full sun plus annual mulching is the way to success. The flowers are pink. This is the parent of an excellent semi-evergreen hybrid *D.* × *burkwoodii* (z6). This is an easily grown shrub with highly scented pink flowers and is probably the one to start with, especially the variety 'Somerset'.

Sun rose (Helianthemum) Flat growing and spreading evergreen shrubs flowering in late spring and again later in the year if clipped over immediately flowering is over. They grow naturally in short cropped grass on chalk hills so are used to sharp drainage and little soil. Give them sunshine and they will flower wonderfully. Varieties have either green or grey foliage and single or double flowers in red, orange, yellow, pink, white and some nice rusty shades. Picking just five to suggest, 'Wisley Pink' has pink flowers and grey foliage, 'Wisley Primrose' has the same grey foliage with pale yellow flowers, 'Ben Heckla' has coppery flowers, 'Ben Hope' is red, while 'Raspberry Ripple' is red and white. z7

Beauty bush (Kolkwitzia amabilis) A delightful spring-flowering shrub, the individual flowers are especially attractive when examined closely, as well as making a pretty show from a distance. Each flower is bell-shaped and a delicate shade of pink except in the throat where it changes to yellow. Look out in particular for the variety 'Pink Cloud'. This shrub thrives on chalk and in bright sunshine. z4

Osmanthus Sweetly scented evergreen shrubs with the spring flowering *Osmanthus delavayi* (z6) being one of the best. Its scent is heavy and penetrating, wafting for long distances on still evenings. A slow growing shrub its small dark leaves and arching growth make it easily recognisable even when its clusters of small white flowers are not to be seen. Larger in every way is *O. heterophyllus* (z6) with its variable but basically holly-like leaves and flowers in autumn.

Tree paeony (Paeonia) Two of the less highly hybridised tree paeonies are excellent choices for chalky soil. *Paeonia delavayi* (z6) is a slowly suckering shrub with very attractive deeply cut foliage which is worth growing for this feature alone. In spring there are also the flowers which are deep blood red with yellow anthers within. Quite a sight. The other species which fits in here is *P. lutea* var. *ludlowii* (z6) which is very similar except that the flowers are like huge buttercups. The many varieties of *P. suffruticosa* (z5) are less happy on shallow soils over chalk but if a sunny site is prepared well and protection provided against late spring frosts they will flourish.

Stachyurus praecox An unusual shrub flowering early in the spring with strings of yellow bowl-shaped flowers hanging vertically from bare branches which are noticeably reddish in colour. The shrub can be a large one with upwardly spreading branches and is very attractive if set against a backdrop of conifers or other evergreens which shows off the yellow blossoms to good advantage. z6

Also try... Aesculus parviflora, Ceanothus varieties, *Fuchsia* varieties, *Phlomis fruticosa, Viburnum* species

Perennials

Pinks (Dianthus) Another group of plants which occur naturally on chalky soils, the pinks are a surprisingly varied group ranging from tiny rock garden plants to the modern hybrid pinks grown for borders and cut flowers. In addition to the flowers, which in many cases are scented, there is the complimentary feature of narrow grey foliage.

Rather than run through a long list can I simply make a plea for the old fashioned pinks? Although many of them do not have the long flowering period of the more modern varieties, most are scented, in some cases very strongly so. 'Inchmery' is a lovely soft pink with especially grey foliage to set it off while the old cottage garden

The pasque flower,
Pulsatilla vulgaris, *is an*
ideal plant to choose for
shallow soils over chalk
or limestone.

favourite 'Mrs Sinkins' is a densely double white with prettily frilled petals. The delightfully named 'Sops in Wine' is maroon with white splashes on each petal and I like 'Arthur', a dark brick red with an even darker centre. z5

Foxtail lilies (Eremurus) On solid chalk or even on alkaline clay soils the foxtail lilies should thrive as long as one or two simple precautions are taken. And if you have a sunny spot and there's half a chance of growing these astonishing plants then why not have a go?

The best varieties, such as *Eremurus robustus* (z7), make tall straight stems up to 7–8ft (2.1–2.4m) high with most of the leaves near the bottom. The top half of these tall stems is covered in flowers in a narrow cone creating an altogether startling effect. *E. robustus* has pink flowers, the 'Shelford Hybrids' (z6) come in a range of shades such as orange and yellow as well as pink and are a little shorter while the orangey yellow *E. stenophyllus* (z6) reaches just 4–5ft (1.2–1.5m).

Chalky soils usually provide the well-drained conditions they like but as their crowns should be planted just below the surface of the soil and they have a tendency to grow out, they are best covered with grit in the winter as a protection against the worst of the frost and against slugs. Other protective measures against slugs may be necessary. Beware of cultivating near the crowns, too; the shallow fleshy roots radiate out for some distance.

Bearded iris (Iris) Flag irises, as they are also known, are one of the glories of spring and early summer but such a brief glory. Sometimes for only two weeks do they flower leaving you for the rest of the season with the stiff, swordlike foliage which is all right in its way but somehow less satisfying than it should be. It's true that by selecting varieties carefully you can extend the overall season but theirs is a rapidly fading flame.

Varieties are available in heights from 1–4ft (0.3–1.2m) and in just about every colour you can imagine. They come in such opulent tones, too. But even after many years of hybridising new varieties are still appearing. You can decide what to order by visiting a garden with a good selection or consulting a good catalogue. This time I'll keep mention of my own suggestions from influencing your choice. z3

Toadflax (Linaria) A couple of long-flowering plants for sunny spots in well-drained, if not poor, soil. The delights of *Linaria dalmatica* can be somewhat marred by its awkwardly invasive habits so a poor soil is advisable, giving it little fuel to power its travels. The foliage is sea blue and the flowers are like bright yellow snapdragons with a pointed spur. It flowers all summer.

Invasive in a different way is *L. purpurea*; this one spreads by seeding itself around. Again, it flowers for most of the summer with dense, narrow spikes of small pink flowers topping densely packed stems of grey blue leaves. The variety 'Canon Went' is especially pretty. z7

Pasque flower (Pulsatilla vulgaris) Growing wild alongside the cowslip on shallow soils above solid limestone this stunning plant is a real gem. It's a rare plant in Britain but one of its best sites is only a few miles away from my home and I never miss it in flower. First you see its dark, finely divided foliage, then the big open, nodding, purple bells. Then it's down on the hands and knees to see the fat boss of yellow anthers inside. Later, as the flower stem extends from its initial few inches, the fluffy seed heads appear to round off the effect.

In chalky gardens it thrives without much attention and can even be naturalised in grass, especially in an open, but not sunny site. z5

Saxifraga This is a huge group and most are relevant in this section so a little restraint is called for. I will, therefore, look at just one group, the kabschia saxifrages. The plants in this group form tight hummocks of small rosettes, sometimes only increasing slowly. Each year some of the rosettes produce heads of flowers, sometimes relatively large, in white, yellow and various pinks. These rosettes then die and others flower the following year, making a self-renewing hummock. They all demand an open situation and sun for most of the day, preferably with a break from it at around lunch time when it's at its most fierce. The brisk drainage that is a characteristic of chalk is also necessary. Some are very demanding and tax even the most expert alpine growers.

But some are tougher like S. × apiculata which is not temperamental and will even make broad flat mats in full sun. The densely packed rosettes are dark green and the flowers are white or yellow according to the precise variety. Another excellent and easy one is S. × elizabethae in its various forms which tend to have a sea-blue tint to the foliage and yellow flowers, often on reddish stems. z5

Scabious (Scabiosa) The scabious so often grown as a cut flower, Scabiosa caucasica (z3), is a fine garden plant too, and especially at home on chalky soil. It's generally a neat plant at about 2–3ft (60–90cm). The best variety, and an old one, is 'Clive Greaves' in lavender blue. 'Blue Mountain' is deeper and 'Miss Willmott' is creamy white.

There are two more which have recently had their names changed and which in theory no longer belong under scabious. The deep blood red Scabiosa rumelica should now be known as Knautia macedonica (z8). It has a typical scabious flower on plants up to about 2ft (60cm) and is very appealing, while Scabiosa gigantea, now called Cephalaria gigantea (z6), is a monster by comparison. Reaching 6ft (1.8m) the flowers are pale lemon in colour and wave in an airy mass quite delightfully. This is a big plant for a big garden — Scabiosa ochroleuca (z3) at half the size is a more manageable alternative.

Thyme (Thymus) Two sorts of thyme fit in here, the creeping thyme, Thymus drucei, for so long called T. serpyllum, and the more bushy type more often used as a herb, T. vulgaris. If you look in a good catalogue you will find a huge variety in various forms from absolutely flat and creeping to firm and upright. 'The less rich the soil, the more dense the plant and the better the scent' is a familiar maxim for such aromatic plants.

Of the genuine creepers 'Coccineus' is almost red, 'Annie Hall' is soft pink and less striking, 'Albus' is white. Of the more upright ones, 'Silver Posie' is a white variegated one with pink flowers and 'Aureus' has golden leaves. 'Porlock' has mauve flowers and is similar to common thyme but is especially strong and bushy. z5

Also try. . . Anthemis cupaniana, Campanula glomerata, Primula veris, Salvia sclarea, Verbascum species

Annuals and Bedding Plants

Snapdragon (Antirrhinum) Once thought to be perpetually popular, snapdragons are now finding their star in the descendent owing to the ravages of rust disease which brings their display to a premature end in some seasons. And other plants have been more greatly improved by plant breeders.

However, I still grow them in most years for the special quality of their flowers and I can recommend two varieties in particular, 'Minarette' and 'Coronette'. They are both fairly modern but grow in different ways. 'Coronette' starts off by producing a single spike of flowers surrounded by a number of shoots in bud ready to take over when the first spike fades. 'Minarette' starts to flower a little later but quite a number of spikes come together.

Different colours in these and other strains show different degrees of resistance to rust so you must find out which do best in your area. None will thrive on unimproved chalk, so prepare for them.

Chrysanthemum The annual chrysanths must give you the most colour for the least effort of any hardy annuals. The most brilliant are varieties of *Chrysanthemum carinatum* from the Mediterranean reaching about 2–3ft (60–90cm) in height and flowering in a dazzling array of yellows, white, reds and pinks often in striking bicolours and tricolours. 'Court Jesters' is the best mixture.

If you prefer something simpler, the corn marigold, *C. segetum*, has a natural elegance which is very appealing and its variety 'Prado' with large flowers and a dark eye is a must.

Also try... Cheiranthus varieties, *Linaria* varieties, *Dianthus* varieties

11

STONY SOILS

THE PROBLEM

Soil that is full of gravel, pebbles, rock fragments or even whole rocks and boulders occurs in many parts of the country, sometimes in small pockets in quite different soil. It causes two main problems.

First, it can be physically difficult to cultivate because the sheer number or size of the pebbles and rocks makes it almost impossible to use tools effectively. Using a trowel in soil with high gravel content is as infuriating as the jarring of the spade when it hits a rock.

Secondly, gravelly and rocky soils are usually very free-draining. On wet soils one of the ways of helping them to drain more freely is to fork in grit or fine gravel but when your soil has too much grit in the first place the water drains through so quickly that the plant roots don't get the chance to use it. Water loss occurs more quickly because the large particles of gravel or rock create large spaces around them — compare a jar of marbles with a jar of sugar, you can see the spaces are larger. Water drains more easily through these large gaps.

This also leads to another difficulty. Most plant foods are not found in the soil as dry particles but are dissolved in the water in the soil. So if that water is constantly draining away to the lower levels, nutrients are being taken away from the plant roots. Nitrogen is lost from the soil particularly quickly. The result is that stony soils are often relatively impoverished and need the constant addition of organic matter or fertilisers to provide enough plant foods.

It's not only plant foods that are dissolved in the soil water. Calcium, found in limestone and chalk and the presence of which governs the acidity or alkalinity of the soil, is also washed out as the water leaches away. The result is that the surface becomes progressively more acid. In natural situations this sometimes happens to such a degree that you find heathers, which hate lime, growing in a thin layer of acid soil on top of a layer of limestone; the constant leaching of

131

the lime from the surface layer provides just enough suitable soil for the roots to take a hold and they never penetrate any further. If your soil contains limestone chips it's likely to stay alkaline in spite of the effects of leaching.

In the garden there can be a steady reduction in the level of alkalinity over the years which may not suit the plants that you would like to grow. This can be exacerbated if the organic matter and fertilisers that you use foster this tendency.

The fact that the presence of stones creates larger spaces for the water to drain through also allows more air into the soil and this can be a disadvantage. When organic matter like garden compost or peat rots, it uses air from the air spaces in the soil. If there is a high proportion of air spaces more air is available to help the rotting process and the result is that organic matter rots more quickly than it does in other soils. So more frequent applications are necessary to keep the level up.

Tree roots can also pose increased problems on a soil that is dry and relatively infertile. Some trees like sycamore have extensive shallow root systems that extract a great deal of water and plant food from the soil leaving very little for other plants (see Dry Shade in Chapter 6). On stony soil these roots sometimes extend long distances in search of moisture and sustenance and create especially large areas of soil which are difficult to cultivate successfully.

ALLEVIATING THE PROBLEM

Charles Darwin discovered that if you simply place a rock on a grass field, over the years it sinks lower and lower into the soil and finally disappears below the surface. This is because insects and other creatures burrow underneath causing the rock to sink and also because the accumulation of worm casts and vegetable debris on the surface builds up the height around the rock. Let this be a lesson to those of us with stony soil.

It's not easy to remove the stones! If the problem is a relatively small number of large rocks such as occurs sometimes on clay-with-flints soils, where there are usually too few to improve the drainage significantly and all the flints do is get in the way of the spade, then removing them when you come across them is probably worthwhile. But when it comes to pebbles and large gravel it really is a losing battle. Better to simply pick them off the surface when preparing seed beds which need a fine tilth and use them as the base for a path.

If your problem is a sandy soil rather than a stony one then the sand is so much part of the soil that you can't really look on it as a separate constituent. Any thought of reducing the sand content can be rejected in favour of lowering the proportion by increasing the amount of other constituents.

But on gravelly soils you can prevent too many stones coming too near the surface by restricting the amount of cultivation that you do. Avoid digging regularly, this will be good for your back and your temper too and, except when planting, add organic matter as a mulch rather than by trying to dig it in.

Of course there are many plants which demand a well-drained soil and if the soil in just part of your garden is of this type then you have the ideal basis for growing alpines and grey foliage plants, both of which grow in similar soil in their wild homes.

But if, like me, you are only content to fill part of your garden with the plants to which it is perfectly suited then the way to create a soil which is amenable to a wider range of plants is to use plenty of organic matter. This serves a number of purposes. First of all it holds water and that is always valuable on soils where the moisture leaches through quickly. It also has the effect, on sandy rather than gravelly soils, of binding the sand together into slightly larger crumbs and so making it more hospitable to plant roots.

Secondly, as it breaks down it steadily releases plant foods which are always in demand by hungry plants. The problem is that as it breaks down quite quickly you need to be constantly adding more. Some gardeners find that a mulch in spring and again in autumn is the answer or one heavy mulch in spring which is then forked into the top few inches of soil in the autumn is also successful.

The type of organic matter you use depends not only on what you can get — or afford — but also on the plants you want to grow. The proprietary brands available in small bags are not usually satisfactory because you need such large quantities that the cost is likely to be prohibitive. Of the types available in bulk, garden compost is usually the cheapest and most easily available material in gardens big enough

Mulching with weed-free compost or peat is a practical way of adding organic matter without forking or digging stony soil.

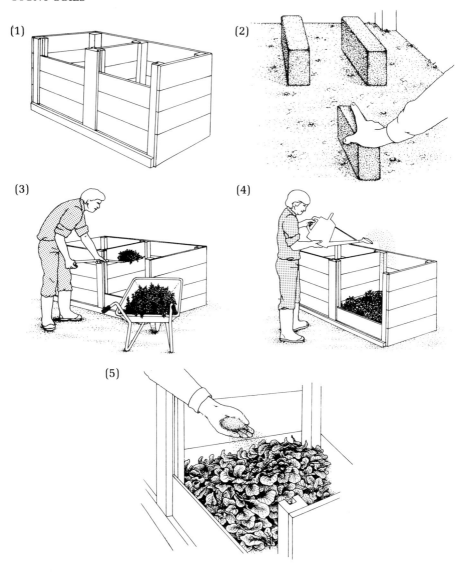

Making compost. *Construct a wooden bin (1) and place some bricks in the bottom to improve aeration (2). Add twiggy material, then about 9in (23cm) of weeds (3) and water if necessary (4). Add an activator and continue to build the heap in similar layers (5).*

to generate enough material for a heap, but it must be made well. If it's to be applied as a mulch to the surface of the soil it's vital that the compost heap heats up well so that weed seeds are killed. Otherwise, you find your mulch is a breeding ground for a vast number of weeds instead of being a smothering layer. If you're serious about making compost get yourself a soil thermometer and test the temperature in your heap; it must reach 140F (60C) in the first few weeks to kill weed seeds.

Farmyard manure is available to some gardeners but this should always be left to rot well before being used on the garden. If, as sometimes happens, you are asked to collect and bag it yourself, take it from the bottom of the heap and not the top as this will be the oldest and most rotted layer.

If you want to prevent your soil becoming too acid, then spent mushroom compost is ideal. This is simply rotted stable manure with gypsum added which has been used to grow mushrooms. It has the advantage of being almost totally weed free and it breaks down fairly slowly. It is available from mushroom growers or sometimes from an agent who collects from a number of growers in the same area.

Moss peat is available in much larger bales than other branded organic matter and is also available loose by the lorry load. This is an excellent material for stony soils as it rots down more slowly than other materials. It is, though, very acid so it pays to consider whether you want to help your soil in its relentless movement towards acidity or not. It also releases very few plant foods as it rots down so you'll need to consider fertiliser applications more carefully.

It has been suggested that clay be added to sandy and stony soils in the same way that grit is added to clay soils, but this is a less practical suggestion. The problem is that clay is more difficult to get hold of and far more difficult, not to say unpleasant, to handle. If it's a matter of improving a small part of a clay garden that happens to be especially stony then it's a possibility but in such a case the well drained area should be cherished as there are many plants that will grow nowhere else.

The application of fertilisers needs to be planned in one of two ways. You can apply a slow release fertiliser relatively infrequently so that the small amount released at any one time can be taken up by plants before it is washed away, or you can apply a quicker acting type more frequently during the season. Wanting to save time on the less interesting gardening jobs, on my gravelly soil I tend to apply a slow acting general fertiliser to my beds and borders in spring as plants are getting going and supplement this with a less generous dressing in summer if I feel it's necessary — for example if there's been a very wet spring. The exact amount to apply will depend on which of the wide range of products available you choose — you'll usually find guidance on the pack.

Whatever plants you decide to grow it will help enormously to give them a good start — by which I mean making sure that the planting hole is large and well prepared with organic matter and fertiliser worked into the hole and around the young plant. Don't transform the soil to such an extent that the plant will not find it to its liking but give it enough organic matter to prevent your having to water every single day and enough plant food to give it a good start so that it settles down quickly.

SOLVING THE PROBLEM WITH PLANTS

Trees

Maples (Acer) By no means all maples are suitable for soils that are based on a high gravel or sand content but there are some of the tougher ones which are elegant enough to make good garden trees — albeit large ones.

The sycamore, *Acer pseudoplatanus* (z5), is an utterly ghastly and pernicious tree with hungry roots and coarse leaves but it has one or two more acceptable varieties. The variety 'Leopoldii' is slower growing than the common tree with pink young growth and pink and yellow speckles on the older foliage. But it tends to revert and I've seen trees with just one green branch — as well as trees with just one variegated branch — so it pays to cut out green shoots. There are two purple-leaved sycamores, 'Atropurpureum' has leaves with purple undersides, 'Purpureum' has purple topsides — but neither has both. Some people like 'Brilliantissimum' with its prawn pink young growth which fades to thin yukky yellow and finally grotty green — to me it always looks ill and it needs a good soil.

Generally speaking the varieties of the Norway maple, *A. platanoides* (z4), are more acceptable and 'Royal Red' and the fractionally less striking 'Goldsworth Purple' are strongly coloured on both sides of the leaf. 'Drummondii' has a narrow white band to the leaf plus reversion problems.

Finally, there is the box elder or ash-leaved maple, *A. negundo* (z3), with seven or nine leaflets rather than the familiar sycamore shape. It grows very quickly indeed — and rapidly gets big, even on poor soils. There are various coloured leaved forms including 'Flamingo' which is almost as unpleasant as 'Brilliantissimum' and the far more attractive 'Elegans' which not only has clear yellow leaves but its young growth has a greyish bloom.

Gum trees (Eucalyptus) For eucalyptus a well-drained soil is essential but the addition of organic matter which goes with planting will give them the essential start they need. This is a huge group of trees but only a few are reliably hardy in most of the UK and northern USA although in warmer climes large numbers can be grown. They are grown for their greyish foliage, their white or red flowers and their attractively peeling bark.

Eucalyptus are best raised from seed, which usually germinates easily, and planted as small pot grown plants as they don't always grow away well if thick roots have become congested in a large pot. They also dislike root disturbance, so if you can plant them from a 5in (12.5cm) pot at about 12in (30cm) in height they are most likely to thrive.

Eucalyptus gunnii (z8), from Tasmania, is the most reliable species and is exceptionally quick growing sometimes growing 6½ft (2m) per year and often reaching about 50ft (15m) in ten years! The mature leaves are curved but young specimens have round leaves which are a lovely steely blue shade. The plants can be grown as bushes, in which case they retain this young foliage, if pruned regularly. Mature trees make distinctive thin heads.

Another hardy variety is *E. niphophila* (z8), the snow gum. This is a much more manageable tree of slower growth with larger, greyish leaves and bark which is mottled in large patches of grey, cream and willow green.

Many species are easy to raise from seed and although they may be killed in a hard winter they often sprout from the base. In any case, most grow so quickly that they will still give pleasure before they are wiped out.

False acacia (Robinia pseudacacia) Attractive trees, originally from the eastern United States, which come into leaf later than many others and grow into attractively shaped mature specimens. They have long strings of pale flowers. One variety, 'Frisia', has become especially popular in recent years and, if anything, has been over planted. It must be said that this is probably the best yellow-leaved tree there is, its bright colour lasting from spring to autumn. But now I would only suggest planting it if there are no others for some distance around.

Most varieties have spines on the twigs and so are not suitable for gardens where there are children but 'Bessoniana' is not only spineless but more compact than most varieties. z4

Also try. . . Aesculus hippocastanum, Ailanthus altissima, Castanea sativa, Fraxinus ornus, Laburnum × watcreri 'Vossii'

Hedges

Hawthorn (Crataegus) The most common farm hedge in the UK is *Crataegus monogyna* (z5) which makes a reliable, dense and impenetrable barrier on the worst soils. It stands less than thoughtful pruning well and can be layered to create an almost solid screen. It can also be clipped back hard to create an effective hedge which is nevertheless very narrow.

Other species have a little more appeal but are a lot more expensive to buy unless you grow your own from seed. *C. crus-galli* (z5) has attractive scarlet autumn colour, *C. prunifolia* (z6) not only has splendid red and yellow autumn colour but also persistent red fruits — it makes a lovely specimen tree, too. Finally, for a hedge to terrify every intruder from mouse to burglar, *C. macrantha* (z4) has thorns which average 4in (10cm) in length. Do *not* plant where there are children.

Eucalyptus not only
thrive in a well-drained,
gravelly soil but warmer
climates suit them well
too.

Sycamores are tough trees
which thrive in many
difficult situations. This
'Brilliantissimum' is more
colourful than most.

Beech (Fagus sylvatica) It pays to be a little wary of planting hedges on stony soil as the roots can help remove what little moisture there is. A dry spell after the annual cutting back can severely weaken the plant. But beech is probably the best as an ornamental hedge. Being an 'evergreen deciduous' hedge, retaining the old leaves in winter, it provides protection from wind and eyes all the year round while not remaining constantly green. I also like the comforting rustling of the brown winter leaves. As long as it gets established it will create a serviceable barrier on the poorest soils. z5

Holly (Ilex aquifolium) One of the best evergreen hedges if a degree of protection from intruders is wanted as well as a good background for other plants. It's not quick growing by any means but it only needs an annual clipping, preferably in mid summer to give time for some new shoots to hide the cut growth. The big problem with holly is that the dry dead leaves have very sharp spines indeed and prove a constant irritation when clearing out the hedge bottom or working nearby. Mature hedges which are bare at the base can be rejuvenated by cutting back hard. z7

Also try. . . Berberis species, Ligustrum ovalifolium, Rosa rugosa

Shrubs

Wormwood (Artemesia) A handsome group of silver foliage plants ideally suited to gravelly or stony soils. They are best in places that get the sun for at least half the day. Some are not easy to overwinter but the well-drained soil is a significant help in this respect as it's the accumulation of too much moisture around the roots and crown in winter that does the damage.

'Lambrook Silver' (z8) is one of the most popular and is tougher than most but *A. arborescens* (z8) with finer foliage is altogether more elegant but also a little tender. 'Powis Castle' (z7) combines the finely cut foliage of the latter with the relative toughness of the former. These all make substantial plants up to 3ft (90cm) high, but for the front of the border the sensuously silky *A. schmidtiana* (z3), reaching just 4in (10cm), is ideal although this dies down in the winter so theoretically comes into the next section.

Barberry (Berberis) Both deciduous and evergreen types can be grown on gravelly soils but the deciduous species such as *Berberis thunbergii* are the most tolerant. Fortunately, this still gives a very wide variety to choose from with flowers, foliage, autumn colour or fruit as the principle ornamental feature but it's the foliage varieties that stand out. 'Aurea' is the clearest yellow in spring but fades gradually as the season runs on; it also needs shelter from icy winds while 'Atropurpurea' is rich purple as the young leaves open, if anything becoming more effective as the summer progresses. 'Rose Glow' has its young purple foliage speckled and streaked with pinkish white and is not to everyone's taste. There are many more including the dwarf purple-leaved 'Atropurpurea Nana', the even smaller 'Bagatelle' and the very upright purple 'Helmund's Pillar'. z5

Cotoneaster The evergreen cotoneasters are reliable plants which range, according to variety, from small trees to prostrate creepers. The creepers are especially useful with *Cotoneaster dammeri* (z5), also known as *C. humifusus*, one of the best. Long trailing shoots which root as they meander across the soil carry small white flowers in spring followed by bright red fruits. It creeps about under bigger shrubs usefully. *C. microphyllus* (z6) is altogether smaller except for the fruits which are very big indeed. This is a good trailer over rocks or makes rather hummocky growth on the flat.

Rather larger is 'Cornubia' (z6), which can grow up to 10ft (3m) in as many years with elegant arching branches festooned in huge bunches of scarlet fruits. An attractive quick growing shrub which is partially evergreen.

Honeysuckle (Lonicera × americana) Not all honeysuckles are suitable for this situation but this one is really special. It thrives in well-drained soil and makes a vigorous twining plant in its full glory in early summer when the 2in (5cm) flowers make a dramatic display for some weeks. The flowers are pale yellow flushed with rosy purple on the outside and sweetly scented. z5

Pernettya mucronata For sandy, acid soils in light shade these twiggy shrubs have few equals. The main feature is the fruits, which are noticeably large for a shrub that usually only reaches about 2½ft (75cm), and come in unusual purplish shades as well as reds, pinks and white. The plants form dense, rather angular thickets and make good informal low hedges. Fruiting is best where a number are planted together; the flowers are small and heather-like but nowhere near as showy as the fruits. A really tough plant available as mixed seedlings or as named varieties with white, pale and dark pink, crimson, dark red and mulberry purple fruits. z7

Tree poppy (Romneya coulteri) This dramatic plant sometimes behaves like a herbaceous perennial and dies right back to the ground in winter or may retain a certain amount of woody growth above ground — making it a shrub. It reaches about 6ft (1.8m), or sometimes more, with tall straight stems and smooth, bluish foliage. The huge white poppy-like flowers have a mass of orange stamens in the centre. It needs sun and is one of the few shrubs that can be grown from root cuttings. z7

Roses (Rosa) Roses will doubtless appear in a number of categories in this book, there being so many types that there is bound to be one for each situation. When it comes to soils which are almost too well-drained for comfort there are just a few that fit the bill.

Rosa rugosa (z2) is a suckering shrub with stout prickly stems and rough leaves. The flowers are up to 3in (7.5cm) across, scented and appear all through the summer. Although rarely making a dramatic show they are nevertheless very attractive and are followed by big red hips. A good informal hedging plant reaching from 3–6ft (0.9–1.8m) depending on the method of pruning.

The low growing Scotch rose, *R. pimpinellifolia* (z4), is a British native reaching only 3–4ft (0.9–1.2m) at most and often only half that. Even spinier than *R. rugosa*, the sweetly scented double pink 'Stanwell Perpetual' is probably the most easily found but there are many other forms. The flowers are followed by large black hips.

Also try... Most grey foliage plants, *Callistemon citrinus, Eleagnus angustifolia, Juniperus communis, J. sabina tamariscifolia*

Perennials

Asphodel (Asphodeline) Its Sicilian home should indicate that the asphodel is not happy in boggy conditions and indeed it thrives in dry stony soil. The flowers of the most widely grown type, *Asphodeline lutea* (z6), appear towards the top of sturdy, upright, 3ft (90cm) stems in late spring and are densely packed with yellow star shaped flowers. The foliage is narrow and an attractively steely green shade. This is an easy plant to raise from seed and has the extra appeal of a strong scent. Don't confuse these with the dwarf and dainty bog asphodel, *Narthecium ossifragum* (z4), which is common on acid bogs all over Europe.

There is also a less widely grown species *A. liburnica* (z6), which is rather later flowering and has paler flowers with slightly longer petals.

Aubrieta Old favourites which, like forsythia, are often decried simply because they are common — irrespective of their value as garden plants. These happy sprawlers are easy to grow, easy to increase from cuttings, too, and are available in more colours than the familiar purple. Given sunshine and this sort of soil, growth will be dense and the display stunning. It pays to buy named varieties as unnamed plants and seed strains are often undistinguished. 'Dr Mules' is still probably the best dark purple, 'Maurice Prichard' is a good pale pink one and 'Red Carpet' is a good deep red.

There are also two good variegated varieties but these are a great deal less vigorous. The leaves of 'Variegata' are edged with gold while in 'Variegata Aurea' the leaves are almost entirely gold. z7

Elephant's ears (Bergenia) Loved or hated according to your whim the large leaves certainly capture the attention either way. Only a select few are suitable for these harsh conditions and *Bergenia cordifolia* 'Purpurea' is the pick. This produces its best colour in well-drained soil as long as a little organic matter has been added to help it in the driest weeks. The large rounded leaves turn a rich cherryish shade in winter and are followed in spring by magenta flowers on stems as tall as 15–18in (38–45cm), although in these conditions sometimes rather less.

Another to look out for is *B. crassifolia*, which is altogether smaller. The leaves are green in summer but the backs darken to red in winter. z3

Ceratostigma plumbaginoides The combination of pure blue flowers with the reddening autumn foliage is irresistible, although the humus suggested for this situation will be helpful. Only reaching 9–12in (23–30cm) the plant is a little floppy in richer soils. In the summer it is, it must be admitted, not distinguished but as the leaves begin to turn and the flowers appear, at a time when the contribution from other plants is declining, it really begins to earn its place. The altogether taller *C. wilmottianum* is less suited to these conditions. z7

Bloody cranesbill (Geranium sanguineum) Neat hummock formers with small fingered foliage, thriving even on relatively unimproved soils. At most the plants reach 12in (30cm) but by then may well be twice as much across. The common variety has rich magenta flowers, there is a white form, and also 'Lancastriense', a pale pink variety with darker veins. All flower right through the summer. z4

One other species is especially worthy of a mention, *G. renardii*. This plant is attractive from the moment the first leaves peep through in spring for they are a lovely sage green with slightly waved edges and hairy, so they collect droplets of water. The foliage forms a neat soft mound and in early summer the pale steely white flowers appear, each one veined in purple. It flowers for many weeks. z7

Perennial flax (Linum narbonense) Another Mediterranean plant bringing its resistance to drought into our gardens. The combination of the rich, though not harsh, blue flowers and the narrow greyish foliage on delicate wand-like stems is quite a sight. It flowers from late spring to early autumn and there are a number of named varieties, such as 'Six Hills Variety' but these are not always easy to find. *L. perenne* is also often seen and there are a number of good seed-raised strains, but it's a little less suitable for briskly drained sites. z5

Gardener's garters (Phalaris arundinacea 'Picta') This is a plant not often recommended for soil which is well-drained but by planting it in a situation which is not too rich its inherently rampageous habit will

The creeping phlox grow naturally on rocky soils and so in gardens usually seem to thrive in similar situations.

be curbed — this may be the only way you can grow it at all. For it really does gad about in good soil, sweeping less aggressive plants before it. This is a grass reaching about 2½ft (75cm) with white striped leaves that turn a dark straw shade in winter. Not to be confused with *Glyceria maxima* 'Variegata' (z4) which has its young shoots flushed with pink and demands a moist soil. z3

Alpine phlox (Phlox) Two species, both from the United States, provide a wealth of attractive varieties. *Phlox subulata* grows naturally on rocky soils along the eastern United States from New York to Florida and is a very tough plant. It makes broad spreading carpets 2–3ft (60–90cm) across covered in spring in rounded flowers made up of five notched petals. The ice-blue 'G. F. Wilson', 'Benita' with lavender flowers and purple centres plus 'Temiscaming' whose flowers are rosy red are good ones to look out for.

Altogether more dense in growth is *P. douglasii*, from the Rocky Mountains, which also flowers a little later. 'Daniel's Cushion' is pink, 'May Snow' is white and 'Boothman's Variety' is lilac with a dark eye.

Sun or partial shade suits both types and a little humus in the surface layer of the soil will help the stems as they creep about. z3

Lamb's ears (Stachys lanata) This is one plant that almost everyone knows, its silver, furry leaves are so very distinctive. In its common form it produces stout felted spikes of small pink flowers in summer at the same time as the leaves rather deteriorate. Two varieties solve the problem in different ways. 'Silver Carpet' doesn't flower at all and the foliage looks good all summer long. 'Sheila McQueen', on the other hand, concentrates on the flowers and disregards the leaves — it has especially fine spikes of flowers which dry well for indoor arrangements. z4

Annuals and Biennials

Borage (Borago officinalis) These long-flowering herbs are being seen increasingly in fields as farm crops now that they are being grown for their oil. And a field of blue borage is quite a sight. In the garden they are easily grown and seed themselves about innoffensively. The flowers come in forget-me-not like spikes which uncurl steadily over a long period to reveal large star-like blue flowers. From a spring sowing they are in flower in early summer and as long as they have at least half a day's sunshine they are happy.

Also try. . . Centaurea varieties, Clarkia varieties, Papaver varieties

12

WATERLOGGED SOILS

THE PROBLEM

There is a huge difference between gardens in which the lawn captures a few puddles after a storm and those in which both lawn and borders are constantly sodden. Many gardens, especially on clay soils, become overwet after wet weather but it's those gardens where the water lays in the soil for weeks at a time, or sometimes most of the year, which can really knock the grit out of the most enthusiastic gardener.

There is only one situation when you are truly lumbered and that's when the problem is due to a very high water table. If the level of water in the soil is naturally near the surface then the soil will stay wet for very long periods, and there is little you can do about it. As a high water table is usually the result of the configuration of the landscape, a large-scale building or other factors outside the garden, you're stuck with it.

Even in an unusually dry spell you can usually tell a soil that is often waterlogged. Dig a hole and you will notice two things — the sour smell and the fact that the soil at the sides of the hole is grey, sometimes with a rusty mottling. The type of weeds growing will also give the game away. Hairy willow-herb, self-heal, lesser celandine, winter heliotrope, creeping buttercup, ground elder, giant hogweed and Himalayan balsam are all likely to be found on wet soil.

The reason that many plants will not thrive in a waterlogged soil is that with all the tiny spaces between the soil particles filled with moisture, there is little room for any air. Some plants have evolved over thousands of years so that they grow happily in wet conditions and these are the ones which feature later in this chapter. Plants like alpines which have evolved to cope with the opposite conditions — deep coarse soil through which water runs very quickly — will naturally last only a matter of days, if not hours, in soggy conditions.

There is another problem. In normal conditions the bacteria which rot organic matter use oxygen from the air in the soil and give off carbon dioxide. In soils with so much water that carbon dioxide cannot escape and oxygen filter down, the shortage of oxygen affects the bacteria as well as the plants. The result is that organic matter rots in a different way and some of the substances produced in this decomposition are harmful to plants which are not equipped to cope.

Apart from a naturally high water table other causes of waterlogging may be compacted soil, a thin compacted or impervious layer preventing free drainage, natural springs, blocked land drains, cracked main drains, leaking ponds, shortage of worms and debris or even the remains of old buildings hidden below the soil surface. Clay soils which are inherently water retentive are dealt with in Chapter 9.

Waterlogging is sometimes most apparent on the lawn but don't get depressed and reach for the phone to ring the estate agent straight away. Lawns which puddle only in bad weather can often be dried out by improving the surface drainage — a relatively simple job. But if the soil down below won't let the water through, fiddling about on the surface will do little good.

In some gardens water collects along the lawn edges, running down to this relatively low area from the soggy border further back. In others it's not until you stand on the soil that you hear the squelch — and then you can't remove your boot without half the border coming along, too. Of course, if you walk on almost any soil immediately after a downpour it's not going to be dry. But if you do walk on the soil, even a relatively free-draining soil, when it's wet, then next time it rains the water will take that bit longer to drain away.

ALLEVIATING THE PROBLEM

Considering that there are gardeners who crave a place to grow moisture loving plants perhaps the first thing to do when faced with a waterlogged area is to give thanks. Somewhere there is a persevering gardener with a gravelly garden, laying polythene sheeting to make a bog garden.

But this is a serious point. Like so many areas seen as problem places you can look at the situation in two ways — you can change it or you can turn it to your advantage. But it must be said that there are few people who want to cultivate moss and liverworts rather than grass in the lawn so this is a wet area which really must be tackled.

If you are starting with a relatively undeveloped garden then proper drainage is usually the answer and will save a great deal of exasperation in the long run. Large gardens will accommodate the small machines which can be hired to lay perforated drainage pipes — always assuming a suitable outfall for the water is available.

On smaller sites it's back to the spade. Vertical trenches can be dug

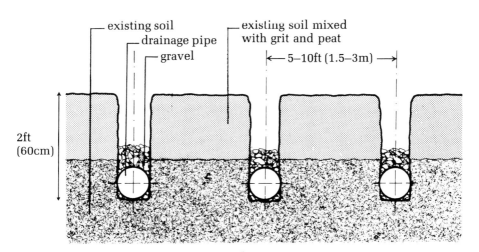

existing soil

drainage pipe

gravel

existing soil mixed
with grit and peat

|← 5–10ft (1.5–3m) →|

2ft
(60cm)

*Drainage pipes carefully laid at the correct gradient with a suitable outfall are the
best way of draining a thoroughly waterlogged area.*

and it's worth buying a special narrow bladed drainage spade to
lighten the work. The trench should be a minimum of 18in (45cm)
deep with a fall of about 1 in 250 and two-thirds filled with coarse
gravel then topped with soil. For a more sophisticated job, earthen-
ware drainage pipes can be laid. The drains should run to a nearby
ditch or a soakaway full of coarse rubble.

In more mature gardens, lawns which only have standing water after
heavy rain are not difficult to deal with. These are the lawns with a lot
of moss and maybe liverworts plus sometimes an especially good crop
of luxuriant self-heal. Lawns such as these can often be made more
free-draining simply by spiking the whole area with a hollow tined
fork, collecting up the cores which are left on the surface and then

Surface water can be drained from lawns by hollow tining with a purpose-made tool and brushing sharp sand into the holes.

brushing sharp sand into the holes. These vertical drainage channels help carry the water rapidly away from the surface.

Keeping the kids off when it's damp is also a great help as not only does it reduce the amount of washing and help preserve the few tufts of grass still struggling on, it also prevents the surface compaction which keeps water on top — but this is a battle many parents are unwilling to fight.

Serious puddling on lawns is often due to inadequate preparation — most of us are in such a hurry to get on with making a garden that we are tempted simply to kill the weeds, rake level, fling on some fertiliser and then lay the turf or spread the seed. But this ignores everything below the top few inches and if the soil is compacted down below water will not be able to drain away.

On clay soils (Chapter 9) a variety of measures will be necessary to create a good lawn but if the soil is not inherently water retentive life is usually more straightforward.

A high water table is the most difficult problem to deal with as you will be taking on nature which has created the rise and fall of the landscape, not to mention its geology. Drainage can help, but improving the structure of the top layer of soil can help too. Mixing grit into the top 6–9in (15–23cm) opens up the soil considerably making it easier to work and allowing some air in along with the moisture. Grit creates larger pores in the soil from which water drains more quickly and into which air can penetrate.

If the soil is simply compacted then digging will loosen it sufficiently to let water through. Compaction is most likely to be the problem when an area has been subjected to heavy traffic, as can happen during building work — even a wheelbarrow following a constant path over soil or grass can cause trouble so always put down planks to run barrows along. A lawn can suddenly show signs of poor drainage the winter after an extension or garage has been built or if there is a succession of wet nights and fine days during the school holidays.

Digging loosens the soil perfectly. Single digging is usually enough unless heavy machinery has been involved. If the soil is basically a light one, traffic will have caused less harm and a rotary cultivator can sometimes be very useful, though you often need a large and powerful machine to penetrate deeply enough. Always take the opportunity to add some organic matter while you're at it, not just because it improves the drainage of medium and heavier soils but the plants that go in afterwards will surely benefit.

The problem can be caused by a pan. A pan is a thin layer of firmly compacted soil well below the soil surface, usually about 9–12in (23–30cm) deep. This prevents water soaking away but can be broken up by deep digging which allows water to drain through. Pans are most common on land which was once used for market garden or agricultural crops when repeated ploughing or rotary tilling to the same depth is the cause. Farmers break up the pan every few years by subsoiling. A tractor pulls a vertically mounted, narrow, curved blade through the soil so that it penetrates to a depth of about 2ft (60cm). You can find out for yourself if this is the cause by simply pushing a metal rod into the soil in a few places and noting any solid resistance at about 9in (23cm).

If this turns out to be the problem under your lawn you either have to live with it or dig up the lawn — unless your lawn is very large and you're well in with the local farmer. A tractor mounted mole plough or subsoiler creates relatively little damage at the surface and can transform the drainage of the area.

If it comes back to digging, then it has to be deep double digging which involves breaking up the soil at the second spade's depth with a fork.

A similar condition can develop if there is a naturally occurring layer of clay in the soil. This will prevent water percolating through efficiently and, in some gardens, if the soil above is relatively free-draining and the land is on a slope, may give rise to natural springs where the band of clay meets the surface of the soil and the water which has been running along the top of the clay starts to flow down the outside of the slope.

Blocked land drains are common in older gardens, especially large ones, and those made on what was once farmland. If your garden has been drained or made on drained land you will find the outfalls along

The new American day lilies like this dwarf 'Stella d'Oro' flower for a far longer period than older varieties.

a nearby ditch or stream — which may not be in your garden. To check if they are clear, wait until it has been raining for a few hours and then don the boots and sou'wester and go and see if the drain outfalls are actually running with water. If any are either dry or flowing a lot less quickly than the others then there is likely to be a blockage.

Unfortunately, knowing there is a blockage is only going to do you a certain amount of good. You can attempt to clear the blockage by rodding the drain, or an expert can do it for you. But if there has been a collapse, finding the place where the collapse has taken place is often impossible. It usually means ignoring the blocked drains and treating them as if they weren't there.

Cracked main drains and sewers can also create wet areas but these are usually somewhat localised. Excavation at the site of the problem will reveal whether or not a broken drain is the cause of the waterlogging but this is not a very pleasant job.

Willow roots have such a great fondness for water that they will seek out the tiniest leak in a pipe and then insinuate themselves into the crack. The roots then swell, opening the crack wider causing a much worse leak. So if you have a willow near your drains, beware.

If it turns out that there is a crack then you will need a builder to fix the drain and a tree surgeon to remove the willow.

Leaking ponds are rarely the cause; usually, once a leak appears the water drains away, the pond is then dry and any nearby waterlogged areas dry out. Water garden specialists sell kits for repairing ponds constructed of a variety of materials.

Candelabra primulas in various shades are natural choices for moist conditions where they will often naturalise happily.

Croquet and tennis fanatics often decide to kill the worms in lawns and then wonder why the surface becomes wetter. Worms play a valuable part in ensuring that water percolates through the soil freely. Their tunnels are ideal channels for water to flow down. Kill the worms, soon the tunnels disappear and then you have a drainage problem. Once they have been killed it's simply a matter cf time before they reappear. On light soils hollow tining and brushing compost into the holes may help, or you could 'sow' the lawn with worms from a neighbour's lawn. Worms from the border and compost heap are not usually suitable and neither are those which are sold for rotting down vegetable matter or for fishing.

If you are determined to grow plants which are entirely unsuitable on a wet soil then the only answer is to build a raised bed. If you simply want to grow a range of plants that prefer an averagely well-drained soil then a soil mixture based on the John Innes formula is ideal. Seven parts by volume of your own best garden soil, three parts of medium grade moss peat and two parts of sharp sand. If your soil is basically heavy use just six parts of soil, if it's sandy use one part of sand. Add John Innes base fertiliser or another general fertiliser at 1oz (30gm) per bucketful of soil mixture.

If you intend to grow the more popular rock plants, use a mixture which includes one extra part of sand; if rare alpines are your particular enthusiasm, then you may need to make up a special mix depending on exactly what plants you intend to grow. Two parts soil, one part peat and one part sand is a good basic mix for the slightly more fussy types. Specialist books on alpines will give more specific mixes.

SOLVING THE PROBLEM

Trees

Alder (Alnus) The alders are adapted especially well to living in wet conditions having nodules on the roots which help bring the tree its essential nitrogen. The familiar alder of river banks, *Alnus glutinosa* (z4), is the one which fishermen find so infuriating as the dry cone-like fruits are a nuisance in ensnaring fishing lines. There are some attractive versions of the native British alder but they tend to make rather ungainly trees. It's naturally a rather bushy and twiggy tree so benefits from a little careful training to make a good specimen. 'Aurea' has yellow foliage and is relatively slow growing and there is a great number of cut-leaved variants of which 'Imperialis' is the most common.

In some parts of California the red alder, *Alnus rubra* (z7), forms dense woods. In gardens its long reddish catkins reaching up to 6in (15cm) long in spring are the main attraction.

Wing-nut (Pterocarya fraxinifolia) A splendid large tree even happy on lake sides. Related to the walnut this is a wide spreading tree, often suckering to form a huge clump of sweeping branches. The foliage is large and generally ash-like in shape and it turns yellow in autumn. If you have the space this is a fine tree tò grow and has the advantage of being fast growing, giving your new garden an air of maturity before its time. (z6)

Willow (Salix) If you have a great deal of space, *and only then*, the weeping willow, *Salix alba* 'Tristis' (z2), also known as *S. × chrysocoma*, is an essential. But please beware for it does get very large indeed, and quite quickly too. There's also the problem of its branches which sweep the ground destroying anything you are foolish enough to plant underneath. But few can resist its huge sinuous branches — given the right situation.

At the opposite end of the scale is *S. caprea* 'Pendula' (z4) which although tree-like in shape never reaches conventional tree proportions. If your small garden needs a weeping subject with an illusion of tree-ish-ness — try this.

Other willows to go for include the slow growing and almost white-leaved silver willow, *S. alba* 'Sericea' (z2), the violet willow, *S. daphnoides* (z5), with its striking white bloom over purplish bark. The contorted willow, *S. matsudana* 'Tortuosa' (z4), is a plant whose effect is diminished if seen too often. A small tree with yellowish bark, the upright branches are curved and twisted. It's a very interesting and attractive tree which captivates non gardening visitors who don't know it but if seen too often begins to pall; so if you already have one nearby don't plant another.

But my favourite is not one of these. S. *aegyptiaca* (z6), from southern Russia, is a quick growing tree in its early stages which makes a widely spreading crown. Its glory is its large fat yellow catkins which appear very early in the season — February and March. Again one that needs a little space but a real gem.

Swamp cypress (Taxodium distichum) The swamp cypress is one of that rare breed of creatures, the deciduous conifer. And that's not all. One of the ways it has adapted to growing in water is to produce what are technically called pneumatophores — but which you and I call knees. These are vertical growths from the roots which stand up out of the wet soil or water so that the plant can take in air. Although most prolifically produced when the tree is planted in water, even when planted on the bank they can still poke through. So don't plant in grass or one day your mower will get a nasty shock.

It's a tall tree, but conical in habit with rusty red autumn colour. (z5)

Also try. . . Metasequoia glyptostroboides, Mespilus germanica, Picea sitchensis, Populus species, Quercus palustris

Hedges

Hornbeam (Carpinus betulus) In gardens which are too wet for beech hedging, hornbeam is an excellent alternative although in very wet soils it too may not thrive. Easily distinguished from beech by the toothed leaves (in beech they are smooth edged) hornbeam shares with beech the useful habit of retaining its crisp brown leaves in winter. In autumn they turn an attractive yellow shade. As an isolated tree the more upright 'Fastigiata' makes a singularly attractive specimen with dense growth of upwardly sweeping branches. z5

Blackthorn (Prunus spinosa) A spiny shrub, much used with hawthorn for farm hedges but standing a little more moisture than thorn. It's best not clipped too often, just once a year in late summer. If cut back hard it tends to sucker from the roots, sometimes in the border some distance away from the hedge itself. White flowers in spring are pretty and there are purplish black fruits, sloes, to follow later with which to make sloe gin. z4

Willow (Salix purpurea 'Gracilis') Few willows could be said to be ideal hedging plants, but if your soil is really very wet then this dwarf version of the purple osier might fit the bill nicely. The stems are wand-like with a definite purple tinge and the catkins are also slim and appear early. Trim in spring when the catkins have fallen or in mid summer.

Also try. . . Hippophae rhamnoides, Physocarpus opulifolius, Salix caprea, Sambucus nigra

Shrubs

Snowy mespilus (Amelanchier lamarckii) Although unsuited to thoroughly waterlogged soils amelanchiers thrive in moist spots. They are beginning to be looked down upon a little following extensive municipal plantings but *A. lamarckii* in particular is still a fine plant with many good features. In spring the leaves open in a reddish bronze shade and at the same time the white flowers open creating a very appealing show. Avoid the pinkish-flowered 'Rubescens' — the colour greatly weakens the impact. There follows a respite from splendour until the black fruits form and these are followed by impressive autumn colour. z5

Bog rosemary (Andromeda polifolia) A short, neat evergreen for wet, acid soils carrying clusters of soft pink flowers in spring. Not flamboyant but very pretty with its pale flowers at the tips of slightly greyish shoots. The variety 'Major' is altogether more substantial and more suitable for most gardens. z2

Dogwood (Cornus) The one that fits into this chapter is usually cut down hard in the spring to promote the growth of attractive coloured stems. Now this is all very well and very attractive, too, but to have to endure a boring bush for nine months of the year for the sake of a winter effect that you will rarely be in the garden to see does not appeal. Fortunately, there are some varieties with additional features. The red barked dogwood (*C. alba*) has, as a constant, its rich red winter stems. 'Sibirica' is the best red, there is also 'Kesselringii' in dark purple; but there are a number of coloured leaved forms, too. 'Spaethii' has golden marked leaves, 'Elegantissima' has white margins and the odd fleck, 'Variegata' has slightly greyish leaves with creamy margins. 'Aurea' with its slightly yellowish leaves is less often seen. Early spring is the time to attack with the secateurs to get the best stems. z2

Physocarpus Not a common shrub but one which, with the appearance of yellow leaved forms, is now being planted more. This is one for moist rather than totally sodden soils. The two with yellow foliage are *Physocarpus opulifolius* 'Darts Gold' and 'Luteus'. 'Luteus' is the paler of the two and tends to fade to green later in the season; 'Dart's Gold' is closer to gold and retains its colour well. There are also clusters of small white flowers in June. They can be pruned in spring to encourage better foliage but as they are not large plants a trim or thoughtful thinning is perhaps more appropriate. z2

Willow (Salix) There are many willows not substantial enough to be called trees although not all are suitable for wet conditions. There are two which are especially striking. *Salix melanostachys* (z5) may be rather a mouthful but what a marvellous plant. The catkins appear before the leaves and amongst very dark scales the anthers are dark rusty red then turn to yellow. A neat stout-twigged little bush it seems to do well in shade. The other, *S. hastata* 'Wehrhahnii' (z5), is also short and stout and produces its catkins well before the leaves but these are silvery grey and then turn to yellow.

Elderberry (Sambucus) The elders are tough plants and vigorous, too. Grow them for their flowers, fruit and foliage and there's a surprising variety. There are three main species seen. *Sambucus canadensis* (z3) is the American version, *S. nigra* (z6) the European and Asian one while S. *racemosa* (z4) also comes from Europe and Asia, but not from Britain. For flowers *S. canadensis* 'Maxima' is the one, its flower heads can be over 12in (30cm) across and the leaves are big too. There is 'Rubra' with red fruits and to cap it all 'Aurea' with yellow leaves and red fruits, quite a combination. S. *racemosa* 'Plumosa Aurea' goes one step further with its deeply divided yellow leaves and scarlet fruits plus its yellow flowers, but this one needs some shelter from the sun or the foliage will scorch. S. *nigra* has a number of forms including the rare 'Fructuluteo' with yellow fruits, 'Purpurea' with dull purple leaves, 'Aurea' with yellow leaves which slowly fade during the season and 'Albovariegata' with creamy margined foliage.

Guelder rose (Viburnum opulus) A wonderful and vigorous plant which does well on many soils which are not dry but which is especially happy and strong in really wet spots. It makes a substantial plant with maple-like leaves and good autumn colour. The flower heads are rather like those of lacecap hydrangeas with a ring of flat-petalled white flowers around a central mass of less showy ones. These are followed by shining scarlet fruits. 'Compactum' is a neat version, not to be confused with the remarkable 'Nanum' — remarkable not just for its dense growth but for its almost total lack of flowers and fruit! 'Fructuluteo' has pale yellow fruits with a tinge of pink — unlike 'Xanthocarpum' with gold fruits.

Different altogether is the most often planted variety, 'Sterile', with round heads made up entirely of the flat-petalled flowers, like mophead hydrangeas, but with no fruits. This is very impressive in flower and even though the red fruits are denied you, there is still the autumn colour. z3

Also try. . . Clethra alnifolia, Sorbaria arborea, Spiraea × *billiardii* 'Triumphans', *Symphoricarpus* varieties, *Vaccinium* species

Perennials

Anaphalis yedoensis Few grey-leaved plants thrive in wet soil but this one will collapse and die in the sunny, well-drained sites that suit most of the others. I have it growing with *Scrophularia aquatica* 'Variegata' and they look great together. The anaphalis has upright unbranched stems with white felted foliage topped in late summer by tiny white everlasting flowers. *A. triplinervis*, at 12in (30cm), is half the height and less grey. z3

Astilbe Soft, plumy heads of tiny flowers on plants from 9in (23cm) to 3ft (90cm) high which love moist sites. These are tough plants which will thrive in many soils and which have attractive foliage with which to set off the soft spires of summer flowers. One other point in their favour is that the dried flower heads of many of the varieties provide interest during the winter.

There is quite a number of varieties, many originating in Germany, so I mention my favourites for you to take or leave as you please. I love 'Sprite', one of the smallest with pale pink plumes over the dark, shining green foliage — lovely. In a larger size, at about 15–18in (38–45cm), there's 'Fanal' in deep and brilliant red and taller still is the pure white 'Deutschland' at about 20in (50cm); tallest of all there's another pink, 'Ostrich Plume'. z4

Gunnera manicata Now here's a plant for a bit of drama. Usually described as 'giant rhubarb' the huge leaves, which I have seen 6ft (1.8m) across on stems not much shorter, are not only big but rather spiny, especially the undersides. Naturally they need a little shelter from the wind to prevent the leaves tearing. Coming from South America this plant is a little tender but the usual answer is to pile the debris from the leaves over the vast rhizomes when first the frost tips them. *G. chilensis* is a little more hardy, but also a little less spectacular. z7

Geranium Only a limited number of hardy geraniums are suited to really wet soil but there are a few. The British meadow cranesbill, now also naturalised in the United States, *G. pratense* (z5), grows naturally in wetter meadows. It reaches about 2–3ft (60–90cm), flowers in early summer but can get rather floppy. It has naturalised itself at the late Margery Fish's lovely garden at East Lambrook Manor in Dorset — rather too well — in a range of soft colours from mid blue to white. There are also some lovely old double forms such as 'Caeruleum Plenum' in light blue and 'Purpureum Plenum' in deep blue.

For slightly less wet spots *G. endressii* (z3) flowers for many months with a steady succession of pink flowers. The modestly sized 'Wargrave Pink' at about 9in (23cm) is the one usually seen.

The wood cranesbill, *G. sylvaticum* (z5), is another European species which has taken up residence in America. Flowering in spring it makes a striking early feature with violet blue flowers each with a white eye. There is also a pink, 'Wanneri', a pale blue, 'Mayflower', and a white form with pinkish tinted buds, 'Album'. For a good ground covering white the 2ft (60cm) 'Kashmir White', correctly G. rectum 'Album', is worth growing and its flowers are prettily veined with lilac.

Day lilies (Hemerocallis) For many years these have been out of favour in Britain but a flood of new hybrids from America has revitalised interest. Although the flowers, which the Chinese use in salads, last only for a day, they appear successively over a long period. The new varieties are generally more floriferous, not only flowering for much longer, 'Stella D'Oro' flowers from late spring to autumn, but in many cases carrying more flowers open at a time. A number of the new hybrids are significantly dwarfer too, and the range of colours has been altogether improved with excellent pinks and true reds as well as the more familiar oranges and yellows. These improvements are bringing a great resurgence of interest in Britain and the United States. Day lilies prefer sunshine and will grow in any soil from moist loam to boggy soil at the edge of ponds. Choose the colours and heights you require from catalogues but look out for 'Stella D'Oro' with canary yellow flowers at 20in (55cm). Rather taller at 2½ft (75cm) there's the intense red 'Anzac' with yellow veining and 'Bejewelled' in pink with white streaks. z6

Iris Many of the irises are suitable for moist soils, preferably in sun. The yellow flag, I. pseudacorus (z5), especially in its astounding yellow variegated form, 'Variegatus', will grow anywhere from standing water to retentive border soil while I. sibirica (z5) is just as amenable though preferring constantly damp situations. It's very upright and stiff yet not awkwardly so and there is a large number of distinct varieties, though in the restricted range of blues, purples and white.

The Japanese iris, I. kaempferi (z5), likes its soil really wet and free of lime but meet its requirements and what a thrill! Hybridised over many centuries first in Japan and more recently in America the variations are astonishing and the colours — every possible shade of blue, purple, lilac, pink and white — are sumptuous.

Summer snowflake (Leucojum aestivum) Once common on the banks of the Thames and Shannon, this is now much more rarely seen growing wild. The easiest of bulbs, increasing steadily, its fresh green foliage appears with the snowdrops and the flowers follow in late spring. Each white bell is tipped with green spots. 'Gravetye Giant' is the one to look out for. z6

The dramatic flowers of
Lysichitum americanum
appear early in the year
and are ideal plants for
the waterside or other
consistently moist sites.

Ligularia Big leaves and bold yellow flowers give a substantial impression in any border. Ligularias thrive in moist soil although they will grow in less damp borders, too. There, however, they worry the uninitiated by drooping all their leaves on sunny days as if about to depart this life, and then perk up happily by the next morning. I like the 4ft (1.2m) *L. clivorum* 'Desdemona' whose foliage is deep red underneath with a tint of that colour showing through with large bright orange flowers in broad clusters in summer. The rather taller *L. stenocephala* 'The Rocket' has much more slender spikes of small flowers above delightfully frilly edged foliage. z3

Lobelia Not the bedding type but tall, upright perennials originally from North America and Mexico with, usually, red or blue flowers. The naming is a little confused, partly by the fact that they have been hybridised so much, but all need wet soil and sun for at least half the day. My favourites are those with more or less beetroot coloured foliage and scarlet flowers — varieties like 'Queen Victoria', 'Dark Crusader' and 'Bees Flame' and the species *L. fulgens* (z8). There is a blue flowered species, *L. syphilitica* (z4), and a hybrid between it and the red ones called *L. × vedrariensis* (z8), which are also well worth growing.

Lysichitum Big bold relatives of the arum lily. The yellow-flowered *L. americanum* (z6) comes from western North America while the white *L. camtschatcense* (z5) comes from not far away on the Russian side of the Bering Straits. The American one has slightly larger flowers at about 12in (30cm) high rising out from the ground in groups early in spring before the leaves appear. The leaves which follow are like banana leaves rising 3–4ft (0.9–1.2m) out of the soil. When happy they can self-sow themselves and if grown by streams seedlings may appear some distance downstream.

Bergamot (Monarda didyma) Strongly aromatic foliage and rings of long sage-like flowers on plants with resolutely creeping roots which are not invasive. If really happy in rich moist soil they may reach 5ft (1.5m) in height. 'Cambridge Scarlet' is still the best variety although there are also pink and purple ones. Seed raised mixtures often have rather weak colours. Originally from America and Canada. z4

Polygonum campanulatum An aggressive ground cover plant for large areas which is agreeably shallow rooting so that if it does become a nuisance it can be easily pulled out. The stems reach about 3–4ft (0.9–1.2m) and are topped for many weeks by clusters of soft pink bells opening from dark buds creating an agreeable dense haze. z6

Primulas There are many species suitable for damp spots, far too many to include in full. The candelabra group which includes *P. bulleyana*, *P. chungensis*, *P. helodoxa*, *P. japonica* and *P. pulverulenta* contains plants in a wide range of colours from deep magenta to bright yellow and will seed themselves happily — and cross with each other – in most situations. *P. florindae* and *P. secundiflora* with the flowers gathered at the top of the stem rather than in whorls are also suitable. The dwarf *P. rosea* with its intensely coloured flower heads appearing before the leaves, at the same time as lysichitum with which it is often planted, is easy and showy. z5

Also try. . . Ajuga reptans, Cardamine pratensis 'Flore Pleno', *Dodecatheon maedia, Petasites japonica*

Annuals and Bedding Plants

Himalayan balsam (Impatiens glandulifera) Also known as policeman's helmet from the flower's resemblance to the helmet of a British bobby, this is a stout and invasive annual colonising wet soil very effectively. Sometimes growing to about 5ft (1.5m) the flowers are pink or white and the whole plant has a very distinctive, some say unpleasant, smell. Easily raised from seed sown outdoors in most areas, it needs keeping in check for its rapid self-sowing can lead it to smother other plants.

Monkey flower (Mimulus) Technically speaking these are perennials but they flower so quickly from seed that they're usually treated as annuals. Recently, new varieties have much improved the selection available. 'Viva', yellow with red blotches is the biggest at 12in (30cm); 'Calypso' in a variety of shades including plain faced, spotted ones and bicolours is a little shorter; 'Malibu' in four plain faced colours is just 6in (15cm) high and spreading. They flower in seven or eight weeks after sowing and so are ideal emergency gap fillers but should be planted on their own merits too. They will probably grow well for several years if happy or can be treated as bedding plants.

Castor oil plant (Ricinus communis) This, the true castor oil plant, is grown primarily for its handsome foliage and can cope quite well with dry spots in the sun. In wet soil, though, it luxuriates magnificently making very impressive bushes. 'Impala' is the most colourful variety with bright reddish purple leaves and its yellow flowers and red spiky seed clusters are attractive too; it reaches about 4ft (1.2m). 'Zanzibarensis' is a taller mixture of shades and 'Mizuma' is a dwarf form with red veins to the dark green leaves.

Maize (Zea mays) The coloured foliage forms of maize are very impressive making big billowing plants in rich moist soil. 'Japonica' has fresh green leaves with creamy white stripes running the whole length while 'Quadricolour' is less vigorous and has additional pinkish tints — which are not to its advantage.

Also try. . . Limnanthes douglasii, Nemophila species

13

ACID SOILS

THE PROBLEM

Problem? What problem? Some of the most choice garden plants will grow *only* on acid soils so you can look forward to growing some real treasures. However, these fall into a relatively small number of groups and there are many other plants that you will probably want to grow as well.

You can check on your soil acidity by testing it with a soil test kit. Simple versions are available and it takes only a few minutes to find out whether your soil is acid or alkaline (limy) and to what extent. The kit will give you a figure on the pH scale as a measure of acidity. The pH scale is an accurate way of measuring acidity and alkalinity in which the figure pH7 is exactly neutral; the higher the number above pH7 the more limy the soil is, the lower the figure below pH7 the more acid is your soil. In natural conditions the most acid soil usually found will be on the heather moor where the pH may be as low as pH3.5 and the most alkaline are chalky soils with a pH of up to pH8.5.

Acid soils can be very sandy, heavy and sticky, or peaty. Sandy soils, even if originally limy, can become more acid as a result of rain washing lime out of the upper layers. Lime dissolves in the rainwater, which is itself slightly acid, and is leached from the upper layers where most plant roots grow leaving them more acid. You can sometimes find lime hating heathers growing in just a few inches of leached soil over limestone rock. As you might guess, soils in high rainfall areas are more likely to be acid than alkaline.

Clay soils can be acid or alkaline, depending on their mineral make-up. Acid clay soils are more consistently acid than sandy soils and are much less affected by rainwater leaching out lime.

Peaty soils are almost always acid and are formed by the rotting of moss or sedges and grasses in very wet conditions. They start to rot but the rotting process does not continue because the necessary organisms

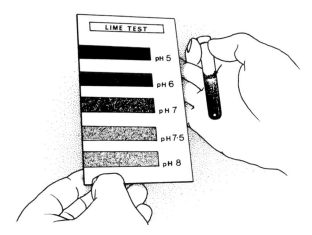

Inexpensive testing kits using a coloured indicator quickly enable you to discover whether your soil is acid or alkaline.

are absent owing to the lack of oxygen in the waterlogged conditions.

Some plants grow naturally in acid soils and most of these are happy in nothing else. This is often because the availability of plant foods varies at different pH levels and plants vary in their capacity to take up these foods. For example, less iron is available to plants in soil at a high pH and less phosphorus and molybdenum at a low pH. Plants vary in their tolerances of these differences. Those in the heather family, which includes rhododendrons and azaleas as well as heathers, cannot take up enough iron from the soil if it is too alkaline; this causes the yellowing between the leaf veins familiar on plants grown in unsuitable conditions. In many cases this incapacity to take up iron leads to the death of the plant unless extra iron is supplied.

When some acid loving plants, such as rhododendrons, are grown on alkaline soils they can suffer from their own success. One of the reasons they grow well on acid soils is that they take up calcium from the soil very efficiently; so in acid soils with very little calcium they can get all they need. When grown on alkaline soils with plenty of calcium they take up far too much and end up with a calcium overdose.

The majority of garden plants are happy with a soil at around the neutral level so in very acid conditions the soil must be changed to accommodate them.

ALLEVIATING THE PROBLEM

Even if you intend to grow acid loving plants the soil may well need improving to enable them to flourish. Sandy soils may be acid but they retain little moisture so additional organic matter is advisable and moss peat is the most suitable type. This has a naturally low pH, usually about pH4, and so will help maintain the acidity of the soil. It also breaks down slowly and so will make a lasting contribution to the soil structure.

Medium grade moss peat can be forked in before planting and the coarse grade used as a mulch after planting. Other organic materials may be more alkaline so should be used with caution if you want to maintain the acidity.

Clay soils retain their acidity but have problems of their own. Drainage needs to be improved and lime free grit can help as can the addition of peat.

Peaty soils often grow very good plants without further treatment, although grit can sometimes help water penetrate after dry spells, and the addition of a limited amount of loamy soil can help create a more balanced structure. It pays not to add too much if the loam is alkaline but by testing its pH and only adding limited quantities the soil can be improved noticeably. I have recently added grit and a limited amount of alkaline loam to almost pure peat and it has resulted in a soil of sufficiently low pH to grow rhododendrons and pieris.

Feeding acid soils needs careful consideration. Some fertilisers are naturally limy and a generous sprinkling of bonemeal each year can have a detrimental effect on sensitive acid lovers. Sulphate of ammonia, which is very acid, is the most suitable form of nitrogen (N) fertiliser; superphosphate is the best source of phosphorus (P) and sulphate of potash for potassium (K). En-Mag is a good general fertiliser which also contains a substantial amount of magnesium.

SOLVING THE PROBLEM WITH PLANTS

Trees

Cornus kousa This elegant small tree is quite flamboyant in late spring when its large, four-petalled white flowers cover the branches. To be correct, it's not the flowers which are white but the leafy bracts around the cluster of small featureless flowers. The colour in the autumn is magnificent too, a startling red and sometimes lasting for four weeks. There is also a soft pink-flowered form, 'Chinensis'. An ideal small garden tree for most soils except chalk but especially at home in acid conditions which are not too dry. z5

Chilean fire bush (Embothrium coccineum) When thriving this is an astonishing evergreen tree clothed in brilliant scarlet flowers in late spring. It's at its best on an acid soil which is not too wet but needs protection, especially from icy winds. There are a number of forms to be had and one called 'Norquinco Valley', which was originally found in that spot in Argentina, has especially dense clusters of flowers. One called *E. c. var. lanceolatum* is reckoned to be the hardiest, partly because it loses most of its leaves in winter so they are not available to be damaged when the worst of the bad weather is taking its toll. z8

Eucryphia Deciduous or evergreen trees, but reaching only to about 40ft (12m) in the most favourable sites but often closer to 15ft (4.6m). Three types are most commonly seen. *Eucryphia cordifolia* is evergreen and one of the largest, especially in milder areas. It's also the one with the least demand for acid conditions although will grow best when given a low pH. The leaves are heart-shaped and the four-petalled flowers are white with plenty of yellow stamens in the centre. *E. glutinosa* is deciduous and, in addition to slightly scented white flowers, has brilliant orange autumn colour. The leaves are divided like rose leaves. All eucryphias tend to be slow to mature sufficiently to flower well and this is especially true of this species.

The hybrid between these two species, *E. × nymansensis*, is perhaps the most widely grown and it has the curious habit of producing both types of foliage on the same plant. It's more or less evergreen and in the variety 'Nymansay' more vigorous in growth than its parents and with flowers over 2in (5cm) across.

They all prefer a moist soil, shelter from sharp winds and a mild climate helps them to establish well, flower quickly and grow to a good size. z7

Snowdrop tree (Halesia) Small, North American trees, or sometimes large shrubs, flowering just before the leaves in spring. In fact the flowers are more like those of the summer snowflake (*Leucojum aestivum*) than the snowdrop. Hanging down in small clusters from the branches, their pure whiteness shelters yellow anthers. An enchanting tree suited to any lime free soil, though a little shelter from cold winds helps prevent damage to the delicate flowers.

H. carolina, from the south eastern United States is the most commonly seen but in recent years *H. monticola* from the same area has been planted more frequently. This is more reliably a tree whereas *H. carolina* is more often little more than a large shrub. The flowers are larger, too, which adds to the display. z5

Also try... Acer rubrum, Cercidiphyllum japonicum, Liquidambar styraciflua

Hedges

Cypress (Chamaecyparis lawsoniana) Reliable hedging plants without the desperate striving for height of Leyland's cypress. Originally found growing wild in northern California and southern Oregon this species has given rise to hundreds of different forms ranging from large trees to tiny buns for the rock garden. For hedging, the variety 'Green Hedger' is suitable and will very efficiently provide the shelter from cold wind — required by one or two of the trees and shrubs in this section — without suffering itself. And one clipping a year is quite adequate. z5

Hydrangea Some of the varieties of *H. macrophylla*, especially the mopheads or hortensias, make excellent rounded, informal hedges which don't get too large and don't need too much attention. They are naturally at their best on acid soil flowering for a long period and following on with the effect of their drying flower heads. Except in very cold areas they can be cut back after flowering, trimming the shoots which have carried the flowers to within a few buds of older wood.

There is quite a range of varieties available in blues, pinks and white and all make substantial looking hedges, thriving particularly in a little shade. z6

Rhododendrons Any of the more robust rhododendrons can be planted in a row and made into an attractive hedge; a little judicious pruning occasionally will keep the shape neat. It's really a matter of choosing a variety whose height is appropriate to the setting and whose flower colour you wholeheartedly approve of; do not be inveigled into making a hedge with 20 plants of a colour to which you are not entirely committed. And don't make up a hedge of a number of different varieties unless you're happy with an uneven result. The dwarfer and medium-sized ones are generally more appropriate as large types can become more open and weighed down by snow than you would like and, if they do need to be kept in order for some reason, are difficult to manage.

As they only flower in spring you may be tempted to think that this is rather less than you deserve. In that case you can plant the perennial climber *Tropaeolum speciosum* (z7) at the base and it will twine gently amongst the branches and peep out with its small scarlet flowers all summer. z5 or z6

Also try . . . Erica arborea, Pernettya mucronata

Shrubs

Heaths (Calluna) All varieties derive from *Calluna vulgaris*, the plant which makes up the vast upland grouse moors in Britain, and many of the varieties now grown in gardens have been found as single plants growing in the wild and then brought into cultivation. They are confirmed acid lovers and lovers of the sunshine too, and all are summer-flowering. Many have the bonus of colourful foliage but varieties need choosing carefully as the colour of the flowers does not

Lupins should be the first choice for borders on acid soil.

The large-flowered evergreen Magnolia grandiflora is best on a sheltered wall.

Some hydrangeas like this 'Blue Wave' need acid soil to thrive.

always fit with that of the leaves. A trim in spring will keep them neat and tidy and when established they make excellent ground cover plants.

Varieties I particularly like are 'H. E. Beale' with long dense spikes of pink flowers; 'Robert Chapman' which has yellow foliage in summer, rusty orange leaves in winter and purple flowers; 'County Wicklow' a double pink; and 'Kinlochruel' with double white flowers. z5

Irish bell heather (Daboecia cantabrica) The most substantial of the smaller members of the heather family, principally because the leaves are broader and the bell-like flowers noticeably larger. Full sun and a determinably acid soil again, plus a spring trim to keep things neat. They have an unusually long flowering season from late spring to autumn. There are only a few varieties but they are sufficiently different from each other and from heaths and heathers to make all worth growing. They mostly reach 18–24in (45–60cm).

'Atropurpurea' has rich purple flowers and foliage with a touch of bronze in it; 'Alba' has white flowers on dark green leaves which sets them off nicely; while 'William Buchanan' has crimson flowers on shorter, neater and more compact plants. z7

Enkianthus campanulatus Alongside the punch of so many rhododendrons some of the other members of the heather family seem disappointing — but only for a moment. Look at the exquisite little flowers of this plant and you'll see that they make up in delicacy and charm what they lack in size and brashness.

Small bell-shaped flowers hang down in clusters, each flower pale cream with pinkish tints. What's more, in autumn the leaves turn the most intense orange-red before falling. It's not a big shrub, reaching 3–6ft (0.9–1.8m), and with its upright habit other complementary plants can be grown up close. z4

Heather (Erica) A huge family with many species and a vast range of varieties. All demand acid soil except E. *carnea* and to a lesser extent E. × *darleyensis*. With so many to choose from it's probably best simply to summarise the qualities of the different species.

E. *carnea* (z5) flowers in winter, starting from January to March depending on variety and lasts for many weeks. All the varieties reach about 10in (25cm) and spread densely if not extensively. Clip after flowering.

E. *cinerea* (z5), the bell heather, has perhaps the brightest range of flowers and tolerates slightly drier conditions than most. A trimming in spring keeps it neat.

E. × *darleyensis* (z6) is similar to E. *carnea* but usually makes larger plants — either by growing taller or spreading wider. Winter-flowering, sometimes even starting in early winter. Trim after flowering.

E. erigena (z7) is slightly lime tolerant and tends to make taller more upright plants. Few varieties, but the recently introduced 'Golden Lady' is the first yellow-leaved form.

E. tetralix (z3), the cross-leaved heath, will on no account tolerate lime and it likes a damp soil, too. The foliage is usually an attractive greyish shade. Summer-flowering, trim in spring.

E. vagans (z5), the Cornish heath, tolerates a little lime and has attractive dead heads even after the flowers have faded. Summer-flowering, trim in spring.

Hydrangea Apart from the mopheads mentioned under hedges there are many other types. The lacecaps are perhaps the second most popular types and far outshine the mopheads for elegance if not in the weight of their impact. The broad flat flower heads are made up of a ring of showy, open, four-petalled flowers which surround a large central area of much less showy flowers. Some, like the wonderful 'Blue Wave', need a little shade to be at their best, others like 'White Wave' are better in a sunnier spot. z6

There are also many less highly bred types which are worth growing and in particular I would pick out *H. quercifolia* (z5), a shrub with rather arching branches of oak-shaped leaves which turn a magnificent shade in autumn and have white flowers in summer. The showy *H. paniculata* (z4) is a little less fussy about its soil and produces pointed heads of pure white flowers in summer after a firm pruning back in spring.

In truth, for most species and varieties, it's a moist but well-drained soil which is more important than an acid one and if planted in dryish soils will usually benefit from a little shade.

Calico bush (Kalmia) Another one of the shrubs from the heather family usually relegated to the second division — but so unjustly. Bright sunshine and soil which never dries out is the key to the most prolific flowering, not a combination all gardeners can provide. If the soil is likely to be dry or the sunshine especially fierce, give it a little dappled shade. Reaching about 6ft (1.8m), the glossy evergreen foliage is attractive and flowering is in early summer with bright pink flowers, which are never garish; there is also a darker variety 'Clementine Churchill'. Along with a pieris, this is the first shrub I'm putting in my revitalised acid bed. z5

Chilean glory vine (Lapageria rosea) A real exotic climber — a west wall is probably best as it likes protection from cold but hates to dry out in summer, so a south wall is not suitable. Its twining growth, reaching anything from 6–15ft (1.8–4.6m), produces pendulous three-petalled flowers which are rather waxy and come in every shade from red to white, although the darker colours are more common. Often grown in a cold greenhouse to give frost protection, it will thrive in a very sheltered spot outside or in mild climates.

This is usually an expensive plant to buy as it tends to be rather difficult to propagate. z8

Magnolia Although if planted in a deep fertile soil most magnolias will succeed in alkaline or acid soils, they seem to me to be at their most successful when given lime free treatment. My favourite is not one of the most commonly planted but *M. sinensis* (z6) is a real gem. It makes a large, widely spreading shrub and, especially if given a little shade, carries slightly pendulous pure white flowers along the branches in early summer. There is a central red eye of stamens and the bonus of a noticeable lemon scent. Looking up at the pure white flowers against a blue sky on a sunny day is a breathtaking sight.

Much more familiar varieties are *M.* × *soulangiana* (z6) and *M. stellata* (z5). *M.* × *soulangiana* makes a spreading shrub with upward curving branches and the large goblet flowers appear before the leaves in spring. There's a number of varieties available and 'Lennei' in particular has large succulent flowers which are dark purplish pink on the outside and a much softer shade inside. 'Rustica Rubra' is a vigorous plant with dark pink flowers.

M. stellata flowers in early spring and is sometimes tipped back by frost. But the white star-like flowers, which appear on very young plants, are a real treat and confirm that spring really is on the way. It makes a very twiggy plant, especially compared with the *M.* × *soulangiana* varieties. There's a pink form, 'Rosea', and a semi-double variety with larger flowers, 'Water Lily'.

An evergreen for a warm wall completes the selection. *M. grandiflora* (z7) has large evergreen leaves reminiscent of those of a rubber plant, and flowers best in the protection of a west or south wall. Given such a site it will grow well and reach the top of the second storey of the house without any trouble at all. The flowers are huge, up to 10in (25cm) across, strongly scented and appear in summer and autumn. 'Exmouth' is an early flowering variety, that is it flowers early in its life, not in the season — always a useful trait.

This plant comes originally from the southern United States and in that and other warm areas can be grown as a free standing plant, although in all but the most favourable spots it will grow more slowly than it will against a wall.

Pieris Every plant in this section seems to demand superlatives and it's understandable that gardeners living on solid chalk are desperate to create conditions where they can grow acid loving shrubs. And it's tempting to spend the next three pages enthusing over the different pieris available; but a selection is necessary so here goes.

All are evergreen shrubs with arching sprays of small, lily-of-the-valley like flowers and young spring shoots which have a reddish or bronze tint. And there the similarity ends. Perhaps the best known is

Pieris 'Forest Flame' (z7). This hybrid combines large pendulous sprays of pure white flowers with bright red young shoots — often in a startling juxtaposition. The young shoots then fade through softer red and pink to creamy pink and then to green as they age. *P. formosa forrestii* 'Wakehurst' (z7) needs protection from cold winds but then produces red shoots and white flowers with slightly shorter leaves.

If you prefer pink flowers then look for *P. japonica* 'Daisen' (z6) with deep pink buds and slightly paler flowers; if you like variegated foliage try *P. japonica* 'Variegata' (z6), which is surprisingly attractive.

Two new forms have recently appeared which don't flower at all! This may seem sacrilegious and I'm not sure yet whether I will grow them myself but *P. japonica* 'Little Heath' and 'Little Heath Green' (z6) certainly represent a departure for pieris. Both make dense mounds of small foliage and the former has white variegated foliage and pink young shoots which appear all summer. The latter is bronzy green. Best to try and see them, maybe at Bressingham Gardens in Norfolk, England, before deciding.

Rhododendrons It's probably impossible to estimate just how many species and hybrids there are and any choice is bound to be highly personal. Suffice it to say that even the most ardent rhodo hater, and there's more than the odd one or two, will find at least a few to excite the fancy amongst this surprisingly diverse group. They range from evergreen trees to small suckering shrubs and creeping alpines. They can be deciduous or evergreen, flower in every colour, many are scented, they may be quiet and subdued or big and blowzy. But all thrive in acid conditions and the majority prefer a little shade unless in moist areas.

Visit a good collection and choose for yourself is the best advice to give but that won't stop me stating my preferences.

Winter and early flowering ones are especially useful, you can usually rely on other people to grow the later flowering types after all.

There's a group of small, early flowering varieties which are especially lovely, although they need protection from the early morning sun or in cold areas need a cold greenhouse. *R.* × *cilpense* (z8) reaches no more than 3ft (90cm), and takes its time, but in early spring carries open trusses of pure white flowers opening from pink buds. Its two parents are the lilac-tinted pink-flowered *R. ciliatum* (z8) and the usually pink *R. moupinense* (z5). They are worth growing in their own right, and the latter has also had a hand in producing some other good early flowering hybrids such as the prolific white-flowered 'Bric-a-Brac' (z8) and the primrose 'Bo-peep' (z8).

Other early ones to look for include 'Blue Tit' (z8) in lavender blue, the deciduous late winter flowering 'Praecox' in shining pink and the even earlier pink 'Emasculum' (z6).

Finally, two contrasting types. *R. arboreum* (z8) makes a small tree in the Himalayas but is more of a large shrub in gardens. A plant in full flower in late winter and spring is very impressive. Shelter from the early morning sun helps the flowers give their best. The clusters of large flowers are of an impressive size themselves and come in white — 'Alba', deep red — 'Blood Red' or pink with deep spots — 'Roseum'. 'Sir Charles Lemon' has especially dense clusters of white flowers and good foliage.

R. yakushimanum (z6) from Japan has given rise to a race of splendid hybrids for smaller gardens all making rounded domes of dark glossy foliage, dusty brown underneath. The flowers, which appear in late spring, now come in many colours — white, pinks, creams, yellows, reds — and a worthy group has been given the names of the seven dwarfs.

Also try. . . Cassiope species, Gaultheria species, Ledum species, Leucothoe species, Vaccinium species

Perennials

Corydalis A number of mostly small rather pretty plants in this group, though some are stunningly beautiful, are used amongst more substantial plants to make an attractive cover. The leaves are mostly finely divided and the flowers, rather like those of a fumitory though larger, are yellow, white, purple or blue. For them shade is the ideal partner for acid conditions.

C. solida (z6) is an easy-to-grow plant with a small tuber and the foliage appears early in spring followed by purple flowers. It fades away by mid summer which can leave an inconvenient gap. C. cheilanthifolia (z5) has soft ferny foliage and yellow flowers but is not so demanding of lime free conditions, and if you want a real challenge then try C. cashmiriana (z6) with sky blue flowers amongst fresh green well divided leaves. This last species needs a humid climate.

Epimedium It always surprises people when they learn that these short herbaceous perennials are related to berberis but a close comparison of the flowers will reveal the similarity. Epimediums are creepers with delightful delicate flowers on fine stems in spring before the new leaves start to grow. In some the new leaves are especially attractive with their reddish margins and in autumn they turn an attractive brown and stay on the plants. If they're cut off when the flower buds are appearing at ground level they won't hide the opening flowers.

There are a large number of attractive varieties, though they repay close inspection rather than long distance admiration. E. alpinum (z3) has small reddish purple flowers and the added attraction of soft green foliage with red tints, E. perraldianum (z6) has large yellow flowers and similarly flushed foliage while E. × youngianum (z5) has white flowers. All are less than 12in (30cm) high.

Gentians For a really exquisite blue few plants surpass the gentians and the autumn-flowering G. *sino-ornata* (z6) is usually reckoned to be the pick, partly because of the lateness of its display. The colour is a true gentian blue with green streaks. The plant is a low sprawler of restrained habits but carrying impressive numbers of flowers for such a small plant. For the gardener who is not a fanatic alpine specialist I can also suggest G. *asclepiadea* (z5), the willow gentian, which flowers earlier on rather elegant shoots about 2ft (60cm) high from which pairs of blue flowers stand up.

Kirengeshoma palmata A substantial plant reaching about 4ft (1.2m) in height with attractive sycamore-like foliage often with a purplish sheen. This associates very conveniently with the clusters of bright yellow flowers which appear in autumn. Sadly, in cold areas this plant can be damaged by early frosts so shelter from cold winds and early morning sun is a thoughtful precaution. z5

Lilies (Lilium) A great many lilies will thrive in acid conditions but I will pick just two of the less difficult ones. The tiger lily, L. *tigrinum* (z6), can grow up to 6ft (1.8m) tall when happy and carry open heads of salmony orange flowers with dark purple spots on the strongly recurved petals. There are usually about 15–20 flowers on each stem though there can be as many as 40. This species also appreciates full sun and a mulch each spring of lime free compost. The other easy one is L. *davidii* (z6) with up to 20 flowers in reddish orange with narrow black spots, slightly raised. This is especially easy to raise from seed and also one of the easiest to look after, though it repays a little extra care in the form of an annual mulch.

Himalayan poppy (Meconopsis) There are far more species apart from the exotic Himalayan blue poppy, M. *betonicifolia* (z7), but it's this that gets most of the attention. Fortunately, it's one of the easiest to grow and is sometimes put in the herbaceous border. It can grow to about 5ft (1.5m) and carries its narrow upright heads of wonderful blue flowers in early summer. Seedlings can vary in their colour but unlike some other species this is a fairly long-lived plant and divisions of a good one will, of course, be the same. Acid soil with plenty of organic matter which is not too soggy is ideal plus thin or dappled shade.

The other reliable perennial species — many flower once and then die — is M. *villosa* (z7). This is quite different with rosettes of tawny foliage and clear yellow flowers; the whole plant is rather hairy. This too is easy to raise from seed and indeed dislikes being dug up and split. Partial shade suits it best.

Ourisia Becomimg increasingly common, ourisias are straightforward to grow as long as they are given a little moisture. O. *coccinea* (z7) reaches little more than 12in (30cm), and above fresh green foliage carries scarlet tubular flowers. *O. macrophylla* (z6) is rather coarser and truculent in its habits though not rampageous and has dense whorls of more open white flowers.

Rhodohypoxis Dwarf bulbs liking the unusual situation of moist but well-drained acid soil in full sun. They reach only 3–4in (7.5–10cm) and over pale narrow leaves appear six-petalled flowers most commonly in rose pink but also in white and other pinks. Flowering time is spring to late summer. Some gardeners cover the plants with glass in the winter to protect them from too much moisture. z8

Wake robin (Trillium) Amongst the most popular plants for acid soil and a little shade, one species, *T. grandiflorum* from the eastern United States, is very widely grown and a number of others much less so. The stems of *T. grandiflorum* reach 12–18in (30–45cm) and are topped with three overlapping leaves which neatly provide a setting for the three-petalled rather funnel shaped flowers in the purest white which appear for some weeks in spring. One of the most appealing plants in this group and agreeably easy to look after. It increases slowly but steadily. It is never cheap to buy — the double form is very expensive — but given a mulch each spring and a little shade is a real treasure.

There are a number of other species worth growing though none quite so impressive as *T. grandiflorum* or so amenable. *T. chloropetalum*, from California, is half as tall again, has its petals gathered into a narrow erect tube and comes in reddish purple or white while *T. erectum* from the eastern USA is sometimes called 'lamb's hindquarters' which some believe accurately describes the flowers. I admit that examining lamb's bums is not one of my favourite occupations but the analogy does not seem altogether fair. Suffice it to say that the blood red flowers are on short stems above the trio of leaves and turned through 90° to face horizontally. This is the same height but a little less stout than the wake robin, but still fairly tough. z4

Flame creeper (Tropaeolum speciosum) Although closely related to the rampagcous nasturtium this is altogether a more refined plant. Small five-fingered leaves and scarlet flowers, each with an orange throat, twine delicately and the flowers stretch a little towards the sun, conveniently, so that you can see them all the more clearly. Often seen on hedges but also good over small-leaved rhododendrons and other shrubs. It reaches about 5–6ft (1.5–1.8m) in most gardens but sometimes a lot more.

Luckily it will self-sow if it's happy but is often difficult to grow from bought seeds and the roots are so deep that it's difficult to move them without damage. z7

Also try... Cardinopsis species, Dactylorrhiza elata, Disporum smithii, Erythronium revolutum, Tricyrtis hirta

Annuals

Lupins (Lupinus) The annual lupins are a sadly neglected race and few are generally available. They are, though, easy to grow in full sun and if the soil dries out they will not be worried. One of the most showy is the yellow-flowered *Lupinus luteus* which reaches 20in (50cm) and is sweetly scented as well as showy and there is also 'Pixie Delight' in a range of soft colours.

Gentians (Gentiana) There's a number of annual and biennial gentians which are not often found in seed catalogues and so need a little searching out. Some are difficult to look after too, but the dedicated gardener might well find the fringed gentian, *G. crinita*, listed and this is worth trying. Its bright blue flowers are 2in (5cm) across and slightly fringed and it can be treated as an annual or biennial. It needs a moist soil and partial shade. Sow in a cool greenhouse and prick out into pots when very small as larger plants resent root disturbance.

Also try... Begonia semperflorens varieties

HARDINESS ZONES
OF NORTH AMERICA

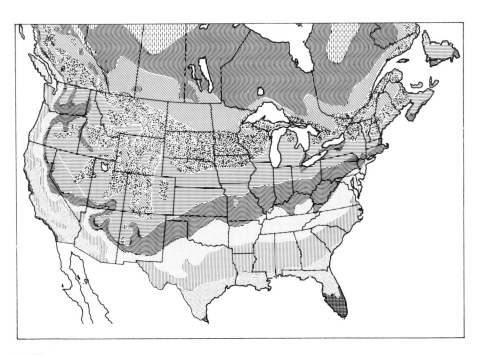

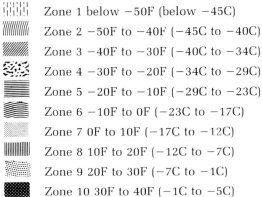

Zone 1 below −50F (below −45C)
Zone 2 −50F to −40F (−45C to −40C)
Zone 3 −40F to −30F (−40C to −34C)
Zone 4 −30F to −20F (−34C to −29C)
Zone 5 −20F to −10F (−29C to −23C)
Zone 6 −10F to 0F (−23C to −17C)
Zone 7 0F to 10F (−17C to −12C)
Zone 8 10F to 20F (−12C to −7C)
Zone 9 20F to 30F (−7C to −1C)
Zone 10 30F to 40F (−1C to −5C)

HARDINESS ZONES
OF EUROPE

HARDINESS ZONES
OF THE BRITISH ISLES

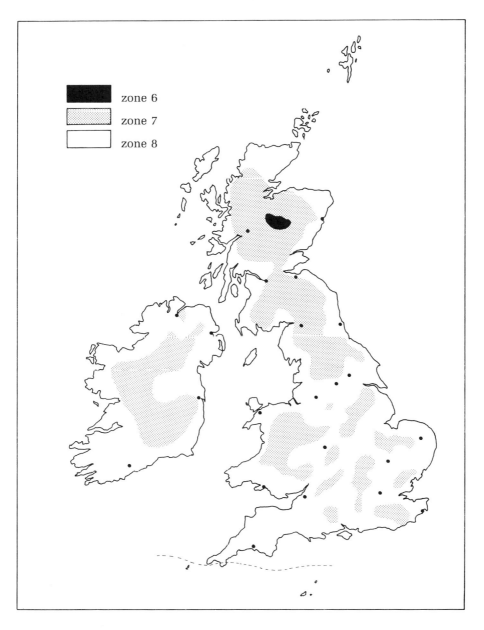

zone 6

zone 7

zone 8

BIBLIOGRAPHY

General

Perennial Garden Plants by Graham Stuart Thomas (Dent)
Plants for Ground Cover by Graham Stuart Thomas (Dent)
Hilliers Manual of Trees and Shrubs (David and Charles)
Trees and Shrubs Hardy in the British Isles by W.J. Bean, Vols 1–4 (John Murray)
The Notcutts Book of Plants (Notcutts)
Ingwersen's Manual of Alpine Plants by Will Ingwersen (Collingridge, UK, Timber Press, USA)
Smaller Bulbs by Brian Mathew (Batsford)
Larger Bulbs by Brian Mathew (Batsford)
A Handbook of Annuals and Bedding Plants by Graham Rice (Christopher Helm, UK, Timber Press, USA)
Flora of the British Isles by A.R. Clapham, T.G. Tutin and D.M. Moore (Cambridge University Press)
Manual of Cultivated Broad-leaved Trees and Shrubs by Gerd Krussmann, Vols 1–3 (Batsford, UK, Timber Press, USA)
Manual of Cultivated Conifers by Gerd Krussmann (Batsford, UK, Timber Press, USA)
Landscaping with Perennials by Emily Brown (Timber Press, USA)
Gardening with Perennials by Joseph Hudack (Timber Press, USA)
Rock Gardening by H. Lincoln and Laura Foster (Timber Press, USA)
Gardening Encyclopaedia by Donald Wyman (Macmillan, USA)
Encyclopaedia of Gardening by Norman Taylor (Houghton Mifflin, USA)
New York Botanical Garden Encyclopaedia of Horticulture by Thomas H. Everett (Garland, USA)

Specific Problems

Shade Plants for Garden and Woodland by George Brown (Faber) op
The Damp Garden by Beth Chatto (Dent)
The Dry Garden by Beth Chatto (Dent)
Gardening on Sand by Christine Kelway (Collingridge) op
Gardening on Chalk, Lime and Clay by Judith Berrisford (Faber) op
Gardening in a Cold Climate by Felicity North (Collingridge) op
Seaside Gardening by Christine Kelway (Collingridge) op
Gardening on Walls by Christopher Grey-Wilson and Victoria Matthews (Collins)
The Peat Garden and its Plants by Alfred Evans (Dent) op

Those marked op I know to be out of print. Copies may be available in the UK from Mike Park, 361 Sutton Common Road, Sutton, Surrey SM3 9HZ. In the United States try Elizabeth Woodburn, Booknoll Farm, Hopewell, New Jersey 08525.

INDEX